To Bartie ·
Margaret
June 25, 1995

I DON'T MIND SUFFERING
AS LONG AS IT DOESN'T HURT

I Don't Mind Suffering As Long As It Doesn't Hurt

MARGARET D. MINIS

CROSSROAD • NEW YORK

1995

The Crossroad Publishing Company
370 Lexington Avenue, New York, NY 10017

Copyright © 1995 by Margaret D. Minis

Printed in the United States of America

The Publisher gratefully acknowledges permission to use the following previously published material:

"i thank You God for most this amazing" is reprinted from COMPLETE POEMS, 1904-1962, by E. E. Cummings. Edited by George J. Firmage, by permission of Liveright Publishing Corporation. Copyright © 1950, 1978, 1991 by the Trustees for the E.E. Cummings Trust.

"The Rowing Endeth" from THE AWFUL ROWING TOWARD GOD by Anne Sexton. Copyright © 1975 by Loring Conant, Jr., Executor of the Estate of Anne Sexton. Reprinted by permission of Houghton Mifflin Co. All rights reserved.

The quotation from Gandhi found on p. 44 is used with permission of the Navajivan Trust, P.O. Navajivan, Ahmedabad–380014, India.

Library of Congress Cataloguing-in Publication Data

Minis, Margaret D.
   I don't mind suffering as long as it doesn't hurt / Margaret D. Minis.
      p. cm.
   ISBN 0-8245-1438-6 (pb)
   1. Suffering—Religious aspects—Christianity. 2. Life change events—Religious aspects—Christianity. 3. Spiritual life—Christianity. 4. God—Love. 5. Minis, Margaret D. I. Title.
BT 732. 7.M55 1995
248.8'6—dc20   95-13751
                                       CIP

"Angels can fly because they take themselves

so lightly."

—G.K. Chesterton

ACKNOWLEDGMENTS

To Bobby, Amy, and Florence, my family, who have been the love and support of my life; to Art Hartzell, who helped me to negotiate its passages; to Julie Firman, who believed in this book; to Louis D. Rubin, Jr., who believed I could write; to Jeanne Garlington, who introduced me to the Bible; to the Rev. John L. Jenkins, the Rev. Edward de Bary, and the Revs. John and Patricia de Beer, who've helped me see God in my life; to Lynn Schmitt, whose sensitive editing has given the book strength and structure; to Claudia Thomas, who's read and reflected with me; to John Kirven, who has rescued me from computer paralysis; to Molly McGoldrick, who's held my hand through it all; and to all the other helpers and companions on the journey.

Thank you.

CONTENTS

Loved into Leaving

This is a book about a spiritual journey, written by a person who had no intention of making one. My main reason for wanting to write it is that the journey has transformed my life, and so I have something to say. I want to say it to those who, like me, are often confused about the whole matter of God and religion but feel a real longing for meaning in life.

I am not particularly good, or spiritual, or religious. I learn the hard way. I have fallen into almost every pitfall and pothole I have encountered along the road to faith, but despite my stumbling I have gotten there.

"There" is not a place I have reached, but an assurance that, as I go, I am known and loved by God.

In making my journey, I have learned a lot about the potholes in the spiritual road and have finally befriended them. I used to want answers to the meaning of life; I have come instead to value the searching for them. For me the blessing of being a pilgrim comes from the discovery that we're all on this journey together and that it ends in coming home to God, who travels with us all the time.

While the spiritual journey is of great importance, I think that it is undertaken too often with a long face, pinched lips, and lots of rules. It's unlikely that someone outside a church community can see any reason to join one if we appear an uptight, unfriendly, and dour bunch as we sit in straight rows on Sunday mornings.

I like to look at the comic side of the spiritual life. I believe that God has a sense of humor, and I have known God's grace most intensely in moments when I have laughed, especially at myself. God delights in overturning our expectations, in showing us we are not big deals, in lifting up the skirts of our idols to reveal their dirty toenails.

Our journey as human beings is also comic in the theatrical sense. In drama, comedy ends with resolution of conflicts, union, celebration; tragedy, with brokenness, alienation, defeat. I believe God has written our human drama as an ultimately comic one. We as individuals may and usually do choose the tragic mode. But God, as the psalmist says, turns our mourning into dancing before the final curtain. We just haven't yet seen the end of the play.

I am writing from the perspective of a Christian, which in itself is a pretty comical thing to be from the world's point of view. The heart of the Christian religion is, after all, an absurdity: Jesus' death on the cross as the victory over suffering and death. Losing your life to find it. Loving your enemies. Surrendering as the greatest power. Sounds crazy! The ideas no longer shock only because the words have become so familiar.

And yet I have found in the Christian story the greatest truth—which I make no claim to understand—that we are loved and redeemed from nothingness by a God who willingly joins the divine self to us in suffering. By no means do I think that Christians are the only ones who have an insight into God; that would, after all, leave out about two-thirds of the people in the world. Christians have just chosen in Christ the easiest way to see the greatest mystery of all: that we, one at a time and all together as a species, are saved from meaningless-ness, despair, and death by self-giving love whenever we embrace it and whenever we practice it.

This book is about the process of loving which has gone on in my life. God has been pulling me out of my self-protectiveness into relationship, opening me like a flower. This has been—and still is—scary. It has often hurt. I am not brave and I hate pain. I would rather *understand* suffering. Let me just talk about it! I don't want to *feel* it, to *hurt*, and I have gone to great lengths to avoid it.

But God isn't content to let me—or any one of us—sit securely on the edge of the dance floor of life, where I can't get stepped on and won't get sweaty or tired, only occasionally tapping my toes to the music. God keeps inviting me to dance, with him and all you others, some of whom God knows perfectly well I can't stand. Sometimes God even takes away my chair.

I can, of course, still refuse: I can say, "Not now; maybe later"; that I never liked that sort of thing; that I don't know the steps; that it's not my kind of music; that I'm tired; or that maybe I simply don't want to do it. The choice is mine, and I will usually choose to sit out any round that looks painful.

That's why God knew I'd need a Savior.

Frederick Buechner says that the reason people like me find the saying "Jesus saves" so offensive is that the last thing we want to admit is that we need saving. When I see "Jesus saves" on a barn roof by the roadside, I shake my head and wonder why the sign painters, whoever they are, bother. It's really kind of embarrassing, tacky. Let people do their own thing; I'll do mine.

"Doing my thing" most of my life has been trying to prove to myself and others how "all right" and "together" I am. The last things I want to feel are lost, broken, out of control. I don't want to hurt or suffer. I don't want to need saving.

Who does? We want to be smart, powerful, admired, loved, thin, rich, healthy, and safe. The problem is that if we could possibly manage all these defenses against the pain of life, we might end up like Howard Hughes: crazy, isolated, and fearful. Spiritual corpses.

The reason I picked the title I did for this book is that I had come to realize that my life had been one long effort to escape pain. Even after I had matured enough to understand that suffering is as much a part of life as breathing, I wanted to quit with that understanding and avoid the pain itself.

Avoiding pain makes sense up to a point. We don't stick our fingers in the fire and we don't step in front of cars. But the fear of pain can go too far, as it did with me, so that we are afraid to risk, afraid to love, afraid to be honest about who we are.

I resisted a relationship with God—I ignored God completely—for half of my life. I started to wonder about the reasons I had done this, and I have come to understand some of them. Avoiding pain was my method, but the reasons were a bit different. Some came from within me, some from without. Some of my reasons may sound familiar to you.

My first line of resistance to the God-dimension of life was indifference. I never even knew a life of the spirit was there, though I had of course heard of it. I just wasn't interested. I went to church as a child, but when I was old enough to think for myself, in college and early married years, I forgot all about God. My imagination was so limited that I could not see beyond where I was. I never began to visualize what opening myself to the spiritual dimension of life could mean. Until I was in my thirties, I lived in a very small part of myself, like a homeowner who spends all her time cleaning and decorating the ground floor of her house, never even noticing that it has a basement and two more floors above.

Another line of resistance was that God didn't seem real. God was more like a fairy tale left over from another age. God didn't fit in with my understanding of the world. I'm a modern, rational person. I understand cause-and-effect, scientific method. I had little patience with mystery. If something couldn't be verified and proven objectively, it wasn't real; it didn't count.

The most powerful reason I resisted God, however, was my illusion of self-sufficiency. I didn't need God. I thought I was fine the way I was. Worshiping God was a practice my parents had said was good for me, along with good manners and brushing my teeth regularly, but I could see more value in the manners and the oral hygiene. I was busy, getting on with my life. I didn't need all that hocus-pocus.

Both my reasons and my methods for resisting God now strike me as pretty typical of most people I know. Get on with life, do the best you can and keep to the high road. My story is sort of a caricature of the human attempt to secure only life's warm fuzzies.

Suffering has come to me anyway. But the fruit of suffering—a loving connectedness to the rest of creation—has come to me as well; it is a pure gift from the God who knows suffering from the inside out.

May you find him in yours.

CHAPTER ONE

The Journey Begins

Although I didn't recognize it, my spiritual journey began in my unconscious during my late twenties. A crisis shattered my sense of doing well; a time came when the old rules didn't work. I had no plans to go anywhere until then. I had cruised happily through college, married a man I had loved since high school, started a teaching job that I liked. I had a comfortable home, friends, good health. I didn't see any need for God. I was like a fat hen on her nest, sitting on her eggs, arranging a few pieces of straw here and there.

And then I became pregnant. My life-changing crisis was a direct result of my own will, desire, and decision. *I* wanted to have a baby.

All my friends were having them. I'd go to visit in the hospital where I'd find the new mother lying in state in a Christian Dior negligee, surrounded by balloons and banks of yellow and pink flowers, a tiny bundle in her arms. It looked good. I'd been married five years. I could see myself in that picture. I wanted a light peach gown with ivory ecru lace. I told my husband I thought it was time. I didn't tell God anything, but both God and my husband cooperated anyway.

Within two months I was pregnant. I bought the gown and decided on a yellow nursery. Bright, happy, non-gender-specific. I didn't have morning sickness. I kept on teaching high school English until the day before delivery, just as I'd planned. My life had worked according to my own agenda for twenty-seven years, except for a few painful times, and I never thought about those.

But as the pregnancy progressed, this *thing* started taking over my body, getting into my space. Watching my abdomen begin to swell, I realized with a bit of panic that for the first time in my life I had started something I couldn't get out of, could not manage and control.

"Wait a minute," I thought. "I'm not so sure about this." At night I would lie in bed staring in amazement at this mound in the middle of me as it bobbed and squirmed from side to side. Kicked in the ribs, I would think, "Hold it; whose body is this anyway?" I felt invaded.

As I ballooned into full pregnancy, I was ready to get it over with. I didn't have the patience to wait for a natural delivery. I wanted it *now*. I talked the doctor into inducing labor, made my appointment for the next morning, and reserved the large corner room at Candler Telfair Hospital.

I went to school and gave a sophomore English exam right on schedule. "I'm having the baby," I told one of my fellow teachers, dumping fifty blue exam books on her desk. "Sorry to leave you with all these." Packing the peach gown in my bag, I was off to the hospital with my husband early the next morning. Just as I'd planned.

I lay down dutifully in a bed in the labor room while an ancient nurse inserted the IV drip into my arm. "How long do you suppose this will take?" I asked her, looking at my watch. It was 7:30 A.M.

"You take that home," she said to my husband, unfastening the watch. "We'll call you when she's ready. It's gonna be a while." The year was 1971, and husbands were rarely included in the birthing process.

After an hour, I felt a twinge in my abdomen. "Great! It's starting," I thought. After about twenty minutes, another. I wished I'd had the watch to time the contractions. The pains refused to settle into any predictable rhythm, however. Sometimes they'd start from my sides and rise toward the middle, growing in intensity. Others would begin and fizzle.

Student nurses kept coming through with stethoscopes to locate the fetal heartbeat. A group of six of them would cluster around the bed, marking various spots on my abdominal mound with green magic markers and then listening to each other's spots. By lunch time I'd had enough. The pains did finally begin to take on a pattern, though, so I occupied myself with being brave and counting them. "Nurse," I called, and the older woman appeared again. "Do you think the baby is about to come?" I asked.

"Pssheet, you ain't seen nothin yet," she laughed, shaking her head and walking off.

By 7:30 P.M. I began to see what she'd meant. Great waves of pain would sweep up from the sides of my body toward my navel and hold me on an edge of agony I'd never imagined. I felt like a giant dog had seized me in her jaws, squeezed and shaken me until I was limp, let me drop. Just as I'd get my breath the bitch would pounce again. I'd never felt so helpless.

The nurse gave me a shot and pulled up metal rails on the sides of the bed. That was enough for me. I couldn't stand being trapped. It was time to take control. In between pains, I grabbed one rail and tried to swing my leg over, two feet of stomach bulging in front of me. "Look," I pleaded with the nurse as she grabbed my shoulders. "I understand that I have to do this. I really do, but I can't do it any more *today*. I'll come back tomorrow."

The rest was vague and I have no recollection of the arrival of my daughter at midnight. The next day I was so drugged I couldn't sit up, and the peach gown stayed in my suitcase while I lay in a bluebird-patterned hospital gown with a sunlamp on my bottom. When I stood up for the first time, my stomach slid down the front of my body like melting wax.

I was aghast. "Nobody told me how much this was going to hurt," I complained to my husband. "Not my friends, not my mother, not my doctor, not anybody. They all just acted like it was no big deal. Nobody told me the truth."

My preliminary misgivings during pregnancy had been on target. It was the first time I'd encountered any pain I couldn't run away from. I couldn't turn it off. I'd lost control.

The process had just begun.

When we brought our daughter Amy home and laid her in the white crib I had painted, she looked very small. I felt even smaller. Our dogs ran in, sniffing and trying to get their noses between the bars of the crib. "Get out of here!" I yelled at them. Would she get germs? Would she die? I had no idea what the rules were.

I went to take a nap, but I couldn't sleep because my ears were straining for any sound from the nursery. I would hear a whimper in the night, tiptoe down the hall, pick her up and try to nurse her, but she had little interest and I thought I must be doing something wrong. I wanted some directions, something I could read, but Amy had no "Instructions for Care" label.

I'd lost control of my time, even of such simple things as sleeping and waking. Night after night I'd stumble out of bed when Amy cried and think "OK, I'm supposed to do this. This is what mothers do." Fathers weren't really expected to help with child care in those days, and I couldn't imagine that I might ask for any help. I had to be a good mother for my baby just like I'd been a good girl for my parents. I was supposed to do it all myself. On the second trip down the hall, I'd start to complain, and by the third time I was martyred. Never had anyone endured such hardship.

My sleep deprivation got so bad that my husband went out one day and bought a water bed, which he put on the floor beside our bed. "Maybe this will help you relax," he said. "We've got to do something."

The first afternoon that I tried it, I had just stretched out and started to float off to sleep when the doorbell rang. Three little girls from the neighborhood stood at the door, smiling eagerly. "Can we come in and see the baby?" they asked. "Oh sure, come on in," I sighed. Sleep was just not to be an item on my agenda.

Sleeping wasn't the only problem. Even worse, I had lost the ability to manage my life. I had been very attached to deciding when I would sleep, eat, get dressed, go to the movies. I suppose I knew that babies did not operate on an adult schedule, but I'd had no idea the chaos Amy's arrival would cause.

I remember spending a whole morning trying to go to the grocery store. I bathed myself, bathed Amy, dressed me, dressed her, changed her. She threw up. I bathed, changed. She was hungry. I fed her, changed her. I dressed again. By then it was time for her nap, and I never went anywhere.

I had been a goal setter. I liked a sense of accomplishment. But now I started to hate people who made appointments at certain hours with other people who could tell time.

Then there was communication. I had always thought of this as my strong point. My customary approach to a problem was to decide what its components were and to discuss them with another person logically, point by point. I had no response to someone who covered my face with strained beets and decorated her hair with carrots.

I resolved my dilemma the only way I could imagine: I went back to work and left Amy at home with a housekeeper. Back to teaching, with ordered hours, structured days, and measurable objectives; I was happy again. As far as I could see then, the problem was the situation, not me. I felt no impulse to change my way of doing things. I just had more things to do.

My husband and I debated whether or not to have Amy baptized. We had both been raised in the Episcopal Church but had abandoned it as soon as we'd started college. We'd rather sleep late. Church seemed too Establishment. When my parents asked about baptizing the new baby, we hedged.

We don't go to church, so let's don't; it would be hypocritical, I argued. I saw myself as daring and honest, rejecting parental pressure to conform. I stayed up on my soapbox. Bobby, my husband, said it couldn't hurt, sort of like covering your bets. He was always the practical one, tempering my extreme stands. We gave in to please my parents, but it seemed like hocus-pocus, something from another age when people believed in devils and demons.

One tiny change took place, though. We became friends with the priest and his wife, who were about our age. We even went to church once or twice after someone called to ask for a casserole for the covered dish supper. Although we didn't realize it, we had begun a new relationship. We had been introduced to a community of love and support outside of our own little world. And not a moment too soon, for my nest of security and control continued to slide slowly toward the rocks that would destroy it.

Again it was a pregnancy that brought the crisis. Two years later I was expecting again. This time I did know what to expect. I wouldn't be thrown for a loop. I decided I wanted to try natural childbirth because I hadn't liked all those drugs the first time. I didn't want any pain either; I just needed a way to control it.

I figured I didn't need Lamaze classes. I got a book about how to breathe and practiced it on my own. I told Bobby he had to hold my hand, that I had the rest figured out.

I went into labor and had the peach negligee ready. Off we went to the hospital, and I lay down dutifully on the table to be examined. The routine again was exactly as I'd anticipated until a nurse moved the stethoscope around on my abdomen several times. After checking the fetal heartbeat, she left the room and came back with another experienced nurse, who also listened. I was pleased that this time there were no student nurses with green magic markers. I was delighted with how well I was handling the pain with my breathing.

The crowd around me grew larger. Five nurses stood there looking, listening. I began to get scared.

"What is it? What's wrong?" I gasped between pains. The doctor came in. He checked me. No one said anything for a moment.

"There is no heartbeat," he answered. This time he didn't protect me with half-truths like he and my mother and my friends had before. This time he handed me the whole life-shattering truth in one short sentence. "We're afraid the baby is dead."

They say the truth will make you free, but first it will make you miserable. I did not let the meaning of those six words touch anything but my denial, which immediately began to take charge, clamping down on the situation as if I still had some power to control it.

"But just yesterday in your office you said everything was fine," I protested to the doctor, as though I expected to talk him out of his observation.

"We're going to give you a shot now. You'll go to sleep and it'll be all over," the old nurse said, looking into my face with kindness. "There's no reason now to go through all that pain."

I remember a rush of water after that and very bright lights. The old nurse said, "It was a little girl, Margaret, and she is just perfect, nothing wrong with her. The umbilical cord wrapped around her neck and strangled her as she dropped into the birth canal."

Perfect. She was just perfect. Perfectly dead. As I floated around in the waves of drugs, I remembered the feeling I'd had during pregnancy that my life had gone too well, that something bad was waiting just around the corner to pounce on me. The fairy tale monster had appeared at last.

My husband and the priest buried the little girl while I was still in the hospital. I didn't ask for any details. "What day is this?" I asked when I woke up. "How long has it been?" I needed to find something to grab hold of, something I could make sense of. I wanted to get back in control.

The doctor came in the next morning with a half-smile. "I'm sorry about your baby," he said. "Statistics show this happens about once in every hundred births. I'm just sorry it was yours." I nodded as he patted my hand, but I didn't cry. I wondered why not, whether something in me was out of whack.

Later a woman I hardly knew came to see me. She stuck her head in the door and asked, "May I come in?"

"Sure. How nice of you to come," I answered, wondering why she had.

"I lost a baby the same way," she said. "I just wanted you to know I understand how you feel."

That really scared me. What I felt was absolutely nothing. What I wanted most was to get home, to get back to work, to bury the experience as quickly and as deeply as possible. What I intended to do was anything but feel the pain.

We didn't give the baby a name. We hadn't known her. I thought of her—it—as something that had been there and now it wasn't. I reassured friends that I was all right. These things happen. I wanted to get busy again. I went back to teaching English part-time so I could be with Amy in the afternoon.

Underneath the facade, though, I was feeling a sense of failure. At that point in my life, having never really had a serious failure, I had the idea that if I read the book, followed the rules, did what I was supposed to, all would be well. That hadn't happened, so I must have done something wrong.

The worst part was Amy. I came home from the hospital wanting to hold her, to console and comfort myself by mothering. She had been expecting a sister and I had let her down. Her three-year-old revenge was to hang on her father and have nothing to do with me. She would not mind me. One day she looked me straight in the eyes, narrowed hers, and said, "I'm glad your baby died."

I lost it. "My baby has died and my other child is a monster," I wailed to our pediatrician.

"Now, now, you must understand how Amy feels about this. Respond to her on an adult level. Think what she needs," he counseled.

"What *she* needs! *But what about me?*" a voice inside me screamed. I felt like a little girl myself. I'd been hurt and I wanted someone to take care of me! Again I felt betrayed: Life was supposed to be different. It wasn't supposed to hurt like this. Just when I thought I had it figured out, had it pinned to the mat so that I could handle it, it jumped back up and hurt me more than ever.

We got Amy a kitten, which she named Clarence, to compensate for the lost sister, and life returned pretty much to normal on the outside. Inside, however, a grief like slow bleeding had created a hole. As if I could fill it up, I got pregnant again two years later, thinking: I'll do it again and get it right this time.

CHAPTER TWO

Negotiating the Detours

All went well during the next pregnancy, but I lived with an undercurrent of fear that hadn't been there before. I went to the hospital three times thinking I was in labor before our second daughter, Florence, was born. As I packed for the third trip, Amy looked at me skeptically and said, "I don't even believe you can have a baby."

I had lost the peach negligee. And the assurance that I could pack my life into a plan.

Florence, our second daughter, was fine, and I already had the housekeeper to take care of her. Amy went to school, and when Florence was two I got an exciting new job as a reporter on a newspaper. I was to work only until mid-afternoon so that I could pick Amy up from school and have time with the children.

The paper was a weekly, started by a friend from high school and his wife. We saw ourselves as crusaders. We wanted to take on the powerful but drab daily paper, which never ruffled anyone's feathers, especially the advertisers. We would tell the real stories. I walked into the office my first day and thought, "I've never had my own desk before." Wobbling between my crusading self and my housewife persona, I debated whether to take the big desk or one of the smaller two.

My first assignment was an interview with the wife of a famous poet who had died a few years earlier. Man, I thought, I was going out in the world, meeting movers and shakers, famous people. I was on my way.

The wife, who had retired to Savannah with her husband, had recently published a collection of her husband's letters. I was to have lunch with her and talk about their life together, get a feel for the spirit of this great man, tie in the local angle. We were joined by a professor from Armstrong State College who had helped her edit the letters.

I had heard stories that the poet and his wife had in years past enjoyed cocktail hour at Bonaventure Cemetery on the east side of town. There, under giant moss-draped oaks, they would sit on a tombstone, watch the river go by, commune with the spirits, and drink martinis, so the story went. I wondered what other stories there were to discover.

We sat down for lunch at a local club, and the waiter automatically served each of them a martini. They insisted I join them. I sipped along on my martini, asked questions, made some notes. A second martini arrived, and the stories started coming out. I wrote faster and faster. By the third martini I was having trouble with my writing, but they were just hitting their stride. We finally had something to eat (I have no idea what) about 2:30 P.M., and I made it back to the office at 3:00.

I held on to the door jamb and took a deep breath. Drawing a bead on my desk, I tried to steer myself in a straight line toward it. As I went past the editor's office, he called out, "Margaret, how did it go?"

I veered into his office and collapsed in a chair. "I think I'm out of my league," I told him. "I need a nap."

Florence learned to dial my number at the paper when she was two and a half. "Mom, Mamie makes me take a nap. And I have to put on my *nightgown* in the daytime!" she'd tell me as I stopped an interview to take her call.

I sent her to nursery school at three. She was pleased to have a place to go like everyone else, only sometimes they made her sit on the green rug when she was bad.

I danced back and forth between job and family like a crazy cook trying to keep the lid on many pots boiling away. One day my editor said he wanted to talk to me and suggested we go for a walk in the park across the street. We sat on a bench and he said, "Margaret, I think you're doing a great job, but I'd like to see you expand somewhat. You really need to be reading the *New York Times* and other big papers, developing a file of ideas, keeping a clip file. Start thinking of yourself as a professional journalist."

I burst into tears. "And exactly when would you suggest I do all this?" I howled. "I'm writing half the paper, taking care of two kids, driving carpools, cooking dinner. I can hardly find time to brush my teeth!" It was easier to feel guilty than to admit that I *couldn't* do it all.

There was one other pot boiling away on the stove: my parents. My father was an epileptic, so since early childhood, between his condition and my mother's constant worrying about it, I couldn't find much support to count on.

I had seen the epilepsy as terrifying. My mother had regarded it as an awful secret and dreaded the possibility that my father might have a seizure in public. Even as an adult, I could not think about those moments from the past without wanting to cover my eyes and hold my ears, the way I had reacted as a child.

I remember as a little girl seeing him fall backward from the dining room table onto the floor, shrieking and jerking and foaming at the mouth. Terrified, I ran to my room and hid in the corner, covering my ears. I could never get away from that sound. When the house grew quiet again, I crept out, looking to see if he was dead. I found him lying on his bed, breathing heavily, groggy and dazed, with a cut on his forehead. My mother was in the kitchen, scrubbing the dishes in the sink with a frenzy. I stood behind her, longing to be held, to know that the world wasn't going to end.

"Mama?" I began.

"Daddy's just had one of his attacks. He's all right, Margaret. You go on out and play. But don't ever tell anyone about it," she said. "It's not something we talk about."

An awful secret we never talked about, even in the family. We were all alone.

At the time my second daughter was born, my parents still lived in the white concrete block house with green shutters in which I'd grown up, right in the middle of town. My mother had developed ataxia, a premature aging of the cerebellum, so that she had to use a walker to get around. Daddy had retired from his law practice to take care of her.

They would sit on their front porch every afternoon, looking at the street, hoping that I—or someone —would come by. My path from work to my house could go right by there, but often I was too busy or I just didn't want to. But I'd see them in my mind's eye, sitting there waiting and rocking, expectant. When my guilt level got too high, I'd go and sit too, tapping my fingers on the arm of the rocking chair.

Then one day a neighbor called and said he'd found Daddy on the floor with his head bleeding. I assumed he'd had a seizure and hit his head.

My husband and I rushed over to their house and found him confused and unable to stand up, so we called an ambulance.

It turned out to be a stroke, which had left his right side paralyzed.

Daddy came home several weeks later, and I was desperate about how to manage my parents' home care and my own family's needs. Finally I found a wonderful man to take care of him. Ceradieu Dor was a Haitian evangelist, and he was very grateful to have a job while he ministered to the people in the inner-city neighborhood where he lived. He fed, bathed, and dressed Daddy, who became increasingly withdrawn, angry, and bitter. One day Daddy even hit him, but Dor just patted him and said, "It be all right."

When I think of Dor now, I see him as Christ in our midst, loving us, serving us, telling us, "It be all right." God was right there with me in the presence of this man, but I couldn't see it until later.

I did my parents' shopping, paid the bills, took them to doctors. I felt myself hanging over an abyss, about to lose control. Never did I ask my husband or anyone else for help. He'd offer, but I'd say, "No, I'll do it," as though I would be diminished by accepting help. I had to be the perfect wife, the perfect daughter. I felt it was my duty, even if it killed me. Every time the phone rang, I'd think, "What now?"

My father, this person I'd most loved to talk to, who told me stories when I was a little girl, would now look up at me, bent sideways in his wheelchair, drooling from the side of his mouth. His brown eyes fastened on me as if to say, "Do something!" I wanted to fix it, but I didn't know how.

Then my mother had a stroke, too, so I had to find someone to take care of her as well. She'd call me at work to discuss whether to have Bea fix green beans with the chicken for lunch. Daddy didn't chew them too well. Maybe mashed potatoes. Or applesauce. That had always been one of his favorites. What did I think?

But it took still one more crisis to make me realize I couldn't do it all. The pot finally boiled over. In one moment all the expectations I had heaped on myself over the years came pouring out, leaving me feeling totally shattered and blown apart.

I was driving my white Oldsmobile station wagon home to Savannah from Amy's summer camp in North Carolina with both children in the car, by then ages ten and five. Bobby had planned on going, too, but a last-minute business crisis had kept him from making the trip.

When he had told me he couldn't come, I'd realized I wasn't too comfortable about going off alone. In fact, what I suddenly realized was that I hadn't taken a trip by myself since we'd been married fifteen years earlier.

I told myself the feeling was ridiculous. I stuffed it like every other feeling I'd ever had that didn't fit into my program. I was a big girl; I could handle it. I turned up the heat on myself.

The trip was fine until I hit a blinding summer thunderstorm on I–26 in the middle of South Carolina. I was in the right lane behind three tractor-trailers,

which threw cascades of water on my windshield so
that I could see nothing but red taillights. For a while I
hung there behind them, afraid to go around, my
hands sweaty on the steering wheel. Finally I'd had
enough and decided to pass.

As I pulled alongside, the wave of water from the
trucks and their noise suddenly seemed to cut me off
from the world. Panic I'd never imagined flooded
over me in waves like the water. I could not swallow.
I could not breathe. I had no center; I felt as scat-
tered inside as the flying droplets around the car. I
was disintegrating.

I pulled off the interstate somewhere near Colum-
bia, S.C., and stopped in the parking lot of a conve-
nience store. The two little girls stared at me from the
back seat, wondering what was happening. I couldn't
go on, but I was still over 150 miles from home. Who
could I call to rescue me? I knew no one in the area. I
had no idea what to do.

I finally did the only thing I could do, got back on
the road and crept along the best I could. I drove the
rest of the way about 50 mph, hunched over the wheel,
concentrating on taking one breath after another. I was
in constant dread of another of these attacks of panic,
which had seemed to swoop in from nowhere.

Amy, who, unbeknownst to me, had been in the care
of a camp counselor who was a born-again Christian, sat
in the back, read me passages from the Bible, and patted
me on the shoulder. When I think about that now, it
makes me want to both laugh and cry. God's quirky
sense of humor. . . . There I was, annoyed at first because

my ten-year-old had been brainwashed by this religious nut, but then in my desperation for any help I could get, listening intently as she read comforting words.

No one could have convinced me at that point that I would one day be thankful for that experience of coming apart at the seams. It was like being blown apart by a bazooka, and I could see nothing in it but pain and terror.

When I finally made it home, all I wanted to do was to crawl into bed and put my pillow over my head. I did not want to tell my husband about the experience; I did not want to think about it or let it close to me again. Awful things had to be buried as deeply as possible. I slammed the door on that part of my mind and piled all my furniture against it.

I started avoiding interstate highways, but the panic attacks increased anyway. I could not drive over bridges. I could not drive to the beach. Always it had to do with driving, when I had to be in control and was most afraid of losing it. I was constantly fearful, avoiding more and more places.

I finally ran out of places to hide. I began psychotherapy. I soon learned that there is no way out of pain but through it. The journey into myself was a long and difficult one. Since it is the very same journey one takes into God, it is also a profoundly spiritual one, but one that I would never have set off on voluntarily. Only a crisis—or a small nuclear device—could have propelled me into it.

The alternative was to keep rushing down the destructive track I was on, gaining speed by the moment.

I was like a train, stuck on one track, pulling a line of boxcars stuffed to the corners with a cargo of anxieties and unexplored fears. Every time I went over a bump, a few more would spill out, and I'd have to go a little faster to avoid looking at them.

I can now see God in this process. The journeys to psychological health and faith have been one and the same. God in mercy let my self-destructive way of doing things fall apart so that I could learn a new way. Unlike my mother, God did not rescue or protect me. I did not set out to change, nor did I want to. All I wanted was to fix my problem with highways and drive on. Get where I was going, make it on my own.

Deep down, what I wanted was to find a sense of security into which I could wall myself so nothing else could get me. But this kind of safety would be psychological and spiritual death. Rather than going back to the womb, it would be entering an emotional tomb. That could not be what God has in mind: God is forever calling us out of ourselves, into loving relationships. Into resurrection.

Without a place to hide, I find myself instead gradually taking down the walls of self-protective control. As I have begun to relax and know myself as a whole person, I have found that I have also come to know my connectedness with God. I am, in my deepest sense of myself, God's beloved child. As I accept myself, I know that I am loved and accepted by God. My energy begins to be freed to love others rather than to protect myself.

I am also better able to accept others as they are, instead of trying to fit them into my idea of how they ought to be, or to edit them, the way I did myself. But God still has to keep teaching me.

My husband and I went to a wedding of one of our daughter's friends a couple of years ago. I listened to the young couple recite their vows and was particularly struck by the words, "with all that I am and all that I have, I honor you." I turned to Bobby and asked, "Do you feel honored?" expecting him to tell me what a wonderful wife I was. I did honor him, I thought. After all, we'd been married twenty-five years; we'd been through a lot together. I thought I had the wife thing down pretty well.

"Not always," he answered. "Sometimes I feel like you only honor the parts of me that fit in with what you want. There are other parts you'd like to eliminate."

I was shocked. I realized it was absolutely true. I saw how I'd graded parts of him as good and bad, just as I had always graded parts of myself. The "bad" ones I'd tried to either ignore or change. I was always working on myself, working on him. That day I began a conscious effort to be more charitable and accepting. Once again, God caught me up short.

I do not think that God "causes" these life crises that launch us on our journey. God does not get up one day, look down from somewhere in the cosmos, and decide whose turn it is to get "zapped." But as we bump along the road of life, pain can open us up to God. It's when we try to avoid pain that we get in trouble. As Carl Jung said, "Neurosis is always a substitute for legitimate suffering."[1]

The wonder of it is that there is such freedom on the other side of the pain. I found that I do have the strength I need so that I don't have to hide and run away. This power beyond what I can summon up on my own, this capacity to grow and to be renewed, what Julian of Norwich calls the "greening power of God," draws us toward God.

I think God is perhaps best able to reach us and draw us close in our weaknesses, our pain, our dreams —the areas where our defenses are down. Dreams can be an especially important path for this connection. For many years I was haunted by the dream of an abyss and the terror of falling into vast space and being lost. I had always sensed it lurking. I would often wake up frightened, jerking out of sleep, grabbing Bobby to keep from falling in and being lost. Out there on the interstate that black hole became real.

One day I read that Blaise Pascal, the seventeenth-century philosopher and mathematician, had at the end of his life the sensation that an abyss was going to swallow him up.[2] The feeling was so strong that Pascal felt he had to cling to a chair to stop himself from falling in. I felt a great sense of relief. At least I was in good company.

Then it hit me: *God is the abyss*—the unknowable, the uncontrollable. God is not the sweet pictures on the walls in Sunday school. Not something safe and secure and containable, to be taken out of a box when needed like the genie in the lamp. God is so much bigger than I'd thought, not someone I could wrap my mind around, but the creator of universes, black holes, quarks and quasars. The creator of me and you and all that terrifying mystery of being human.

I worked on this. If God is the abyss, then it is all right to fall, because what we fall into is love. I am loved by something so much vaster than I can ever imagine, greater than the categories of good and bad by which I judge myself and others, uniting them in a wholeness beyond the power of any earthly fusion.

I truly believe this. So do I stand on the edge of this abyss which is God and leap happily into it, knowing that I will be sustained as I tumble down? Hell no. I look over, retreat from the edge, from God and from myself, I scramble for the place I used to be: I call for help from my friends.

No matter. God expects such behavior from me and from most of us. God will help me over the edge no matter how much I scramble away. I imagine divine laughter at the way I try to hang on to the weeds, rocks, and even cacti on the precipice. They don't help me; they cut my hands as they slide through, but I grab hold even harder. It's only when I've lost my last hold and know that I am lost that I hear God saying, "You see, I had you all along."

A marvelous parallel for this is in the Gospel of Luke. When Jesus confronts a naked demoniac who lives wild and alone among the tombs, the man cries out, "What have you to do with me, Jesus, Son of the Most High God?"

The crazy man senses, as we all do when confronted with the light and life of God, his own deadness. He is naked, defenseless. He knows the awful gulf between himself and the holy. How can God have anything to do with him?

We also run from what can save us because we can't stand to be naked, to see the truth about ourselves. We also feel the awful gulf between ourselves and the holiness of God. Sometimes we have to feel a little crazy to reach out.

The demons inside the crazy man beg Jesus not to command them to depart into the *abyss*, opting instead to inhabit a herd of pigs! How like me. I often shrink from the holiness of God, feeling it has nothing to do with me. I would rather live with my familiar demons among the dead parts of myself in almost any secure and nearby spiritual wallow, than to throw away my fear and fall over the edge, into the mystery of God, the abyss.

Who wants to "Let go and let God"? A student in the school of suffering said it best: "Everything I ever let go of had my claw marks all over it!"[3]

CHAPTER THREE

Going My Way

My own scrambling back from the edge of the abyss of God has taken many forms, most of them about as ridiculous as begging to live in a herd of pigs. I notice that the demons in Luke's story didn't escape even by this tactic, however. The pigs took them over the edge anyway.

So it has been with most of my escapes: They didn't work in the long run because God didn't give up on me, and God has a lot more endurance and time than I do. My efforts to escape aren't even particularly new or original. I suspect (and hope) that readers will find some of them familiar.

The first one I call filling in. Spiritual writers have described a "God-shaped emptiness inside us" which we try to fill with anything we can think of, but which is satisfied only with God. I have often used this filling-in approach to avoid God. I have a sneaking sense of my own emptiness; it's not a very comfortable feeling. I don't like the way it feels, so I try to fill it up. I face it squarely only when I sit down to write, in times when I am alone and quiet.

One of my methods of scrambling away from this God-shaped emptiness takes the form of thinking, "If I only had _____ , everything would be all right." I have pushed many things into that blank, like a bull-dozer working a borrow pit. My fillers are legion, and, like the demons in Luke's story of the crazy man, they have made me only more frantic, and never filled.

The first filler is money. I grew up never having what I thought was enough. I went to college on a scholarship and always had a stack of bills on my desk. I remember sorting through them, debating which was the most urgent, telling myself, "If I only had enough money to pay them all, I would be happy."

I got married and went to work as a teacher. My husband was a stockbroker. We had no children and an ample income. But the stack of bills was still there, only higher now because we had an apartment, a small boat, a dog, and two charge cards. I remember thinking, "If I only had another $100 a month, everything would be all right."

Then there were two children in private school, a house, two dogs, two cats, three boats, and two cars. I had two jobs with different newspapers. My husband was selling boats and had another job as well. We each had a wallet full of credit cards. I bought a desk organizer with three shelves for the bills. I was beginning to catch on. There was never going to be enough money because the hole of my wants kept getting bigger and bigger.

I remember some years ago reading Judy Blume's book, *Are You There, God? It's Me, Margaret.* The little girl who tells the story says she feels like a giant piece of Swiss cheese, full of huge holes which she keeps trying to fill up. I knew just what she meant.

Another hole-plugger I've tried is activity. The way this works is that I stay so busy I don't notice the emptiness. I did this in a programmed way, categorizing the things I needed to do into exercise, work, community service, family, and friends. I played tennis, ran to work, drove carpools, visited my parents, went to board meetings, served on committees, cooked dinner, read stories, gave dinner parties, made love. Before I ever opened my eyes in the morning, I would be composing a list of what had to be accomplished that day. I felt like a circus animal jumping through hoops, but I never stopped to ask who was holding the hoops. I was too busy to wonder.

One day my dog threw up on the floor and I burst into tears. I simply couldn't fit a trip to the vet into all the things I "had" to do that day.

I found myself having fantasies of getting sick and going to the hospital where everyone would come to visit me and bring me flowers. I wouldn't have to *do* anything. Not a spa, mind you, where I chose to do nothing. That would threaten my image of myself as a virtuous hard worker. My respite would have to be inflicted on me.

Another strategy pops up here. Reputation. If enough other people thought I was hard-working, virtuous, upright, and honest, then it must be true, despite the unworthiness I knew inside. I treasured people's admiration and praise and stuffed them into my empty place. I was very defensive if anyone criticized something I had done. When people didn't think I was wonderful, then maybe I was as empty as I feared. The abyss loomed relentlessly despite all the plaudits I could shove into it.

Another good way to avoid God is to try to be God yourself, or at least to play at it. Better to *be* God than to *let* God!

This escape from God is as old as Adam and Eve. In the story in Genesis, the archetypal couple, with a little push from the snake, decide to take matters into their own hands, eat the fruit, and know the whole story like the Old Man. They'll do it their way. They will be like God.

But it backfires. The first thing they know is their own nakedness, their own creatureliness.

My particular version of playing God had a Trinitarian form. First I assumed the role as my own creator— not literally of course, but in the self I created to present to the world. I worked very hard even as an adult to convince everyone else and myself that I was the good girl that I had been when I was playing this game with my parents.

My parents had given me good training for this, applauding my act, not wanting to know the whole story about me any more than I did. They wanted a good girl, and that's what they got. Both sides in this pact understood that there was a lot we didn't ever talk about. We all did a lot of hiding.

Despite my efforts to create myself in the image of a good girl, I screwed up. I found I had lots of other desires that didn't fit in. I discovered myself, as Paul says, doing not what I wanted but what I hated. He explains this perfectly in Romans: "I can will what is right, but I cannot do it." So then what? I needed a savior.

I undertook the job myself, moving into the second role of the Trinity, the Savior. I could redeem myself from the bad things I do, I figured at some level, if I do as many or more good things. Balance-sheet spirituality. God will look down my page in the heavenly ledger and will be impressed because the credits outnumber the debits. I started going to church. I taught Sunday school (even though I could have killed the little monsters without a qualm most Sunday mornings). I worked at the hospital as a volunteer, dispensing flowers and benevolence. I gave up smoking. I was nicer to my mother. I wrote thank-you notes promptly.

The problem with all this was that it wore me out. I had to be my own Holy Spirit as well, summoning up all the energy to keep up my good works, the source of all the love and goodness dispensed. I was solely responsible for everything that happened to me. I was the one who had to make it turn out OK, the Sanctifier of my own life. It was all up to me. No wonder I got a little anxious.

This next escape hatch is a bit more intellectual: *via negativa*, thinking about what God is not. The term *via negativa* describes a theological process of trying to explain what God is not, since it is so hard to explain what God is. He is not, for instance, measurable, knowable, limited by time and space. He is not even "he"! The problem with this approach is that it leaves you knowing no more about God than you did when you started.

I have used it, nevertheless, as another escape from God: If I talk about him enough, I may never have to meet him. The approach is also very popular with academics and theologians.

Reductionism might be a better term for it. I reduce God to something more manageable by checking off all the things he is not, leaving me something easier to work with. Or leaving me with nothing so I don't have to bother with him. I can play this game with other people too, boxing them into the categories of my own thinking instead of seeing them in their wholeness as God created them. I can even play alone, reducing myself to insignificance so nothing is expected of me.

Let me begin with myself since that's where I spend a lot of time. I am not a painter, a musician, a skier, a dancer, an astronaut. I am no longer a teacher, nor a journalist, and my term of active mothering is fast running out. I am not a good girl, I've discovered, nor even a particularly unusual person. People ask what I do and I have a hard time explaining. I've lost the labels by which I used to categorize myself. If I'm just what I do—a "human doing"— maybe I'm not much at all.

Another example: My neighbor across the street is not rich, famous, or socially prominent. He's not good looking, industrious, or involved in any community activities. He doesn't pay any attention to me when I walk by his house, so he's not friendly. Obviously, I don't owe him consideration. He must not be worth my bothering with him.

God is not a voice I can hear. God does not appear to me on the road to Damascus or Detroit or anywhere else. God does not answer my prayers in a way that I can be sure whether God did it or not. God is not consistent: sometimes healing, sometimes letting the innocent suffer, sometimes allowing my dog to be hit by a car. God's world does not work the way I think it should. God is not fair; God does not seem to reward virtue and punish vice the way I was told as a child that God would. God does not play by my rules, so what good is God? I'll pick up my marbles and go home.

If that one sounds sort of childish, this one is even better: seeing God as Big Daddy.

This sort of childish attitude pops up as another reason we run away from God: We imagine God as a giant version of our parents. Just like we did when we were children, we try to see what we can get away with. We giggle to ourselves as we expriment with various forms of sin—all of them about as original as trying to feed the green beans to the dog under the table—and think we have really put one over on the Old Man.

I heard a wonderful story that illustrates this. There was a rich man who decided one day to do something nice for the poor carpenter who lived down the street. He knocked at the door, and the carpenter emerged, a trail of snotty-nosed whining children behind him.

"Good morning," the rich man said. "I would like to hire you to build me a house. Here are the plans. Here is enough money to complete the job. I want it to be the finest house possible, made with all the best materials. Hire the most skillful craftsmen and do your best work. I'm leaving you in charge, as I am going on a long journey and will not return until the house is finished."

"Don't worry, sir, I'll handle it," the carpenter replied, his face lighting up. He took the money—more than he had ever seen in his life— and went back inside to tell his wife.

They figured this was their big chance. The carpenter bought all seconds instead of the finest materials. He hired sleazy workmen and painted over their mistakes. He left things out and took shortcuts. The carpenter and his wife squirreled away half the money and planned a trip to Vegas, where they could gamble and get twice as much.

The rich man came back and knocked at the door. The carpenter was a little nervous. "I've finished the job, sir, just like you asked. The house is built, and here are the keys. It's ready for you to move in."

The rich man smiled and his eyes were kind and filled with love. "No," he said as he handed the keys back to the carpenter, "you keep the keys. I built the house for you." [1]

It's sort of like growing up and finding you hadn't been fooling your parents all along. I have had much better luck at fooling myself.

One of the most pernicious ways I have used to exclude God from my life while searching for him has been to try to be "normal." Here's how it works: I ask God to make himself known to me, to enter my life, but when he does I hurry back to where I was because I don't want to be different from everybody else. The very last thing I want anyone to say about me is that I am weird, a "religious nut."

I figure out what I should be doing by looking around at everybody else to see what's normal and then I fit myself into the pattern. It's sort of like the way my daughter used to dance in a ballet recital when she was five years old: she would hold her hands gracefully over her head and look at the person next to her to know when to point or hop. She was always half a hop behind and never moved by the music.

My need to fit in didn't leave much space in my life for God. He could speak in hushed tones while the organ was playing at the Sunday morning service. He could answer me when I called, sort of like a celestial butler, but he was not to speak unless spoken to. God could reward me with good feelings about myself when I gave away clothes and my old stereo to the poor. God could enter my intellect through books and discussions with other polite, well-intentioned searchers. These debates could never be heated though, because, after all, such questions about God had no sure-fire answers; the discussions were sort of metaphysical fly-casting contests where dexterity counted most.

My rules of contact with God did not include anything indicated in biblical models of human–divine interaction. No all-night wrestling in the dark. No being sent off into unknown lands with no answers and no directions other than "Follow me." No working all day in the vineyard to find that I hadn't earned any more than the late arrivals.

And certainly what I most of all did *not* want from God were the things (the spiritual gifts) described by the apostle Paul as being precisely what God was eager to give: healing, prophecy, speaking in tongues or interpreting them—though maybe a little teaching would have been acceptable. Whatever was beyond my control God could keep. I wasn't sure I believed in all that sort of stuff anyway, and I sure as hell didn't want to be around anybody that did. My mother had told me about "Holy Rollers," and I was glad I had grown up in the Episcopal Church, where even singing above a whisper was looked on askance in those days.

In the Deep Southern family in which I grew up, the worst thing that somebody could say about you was that you were tacky, which included wearing flashy clothes or jewelry, driving big, bright cars, talking too loudly at parties, and wearing too much make-up. If you had money, everyone could know, but it shouldn't show except in antiques, silver, Oriental rugs, and lovely homes hidden beneath large trees.

A Southern Lady is to be gracious, pleasing to everyone, above sweating or other bodily functions, serene, kind, and without strong opinions or desires. Lovely.

While I always had a hard time with this image, I still had it implanted in my mind as what I should be working toward; it continued to function as my warped idea of "normal." It produced a sort of schizophrenia, in which I tried to act like a lady around my parents and to have fun on the sly. Never did it occur to me that finding out who I was was might be fun or that anyone might like me if they knew the real thing.

My limited view of what it was OK to be fit in with my limited relationship with God. Somehow I knew that if God got too close, God would start rearranging things inside. And that might mean the worst of all possible results: not only would people talk about me, but I might be a different person.

I see things from quite a different perspective now, but if I never speak in tongues that's just fine with me. I am still afraid when I talk of my faith in the cold, cruel world. But I'm learning. So what if they look at me funny?

Running away from God is another time-tried way I've used to escape. Again, it's not original, going back to Adam and Eve and practiced by a long line of humans from Jonah to the inhabitants of Jerusalem. Saul hid in the baggage when God chose him to be king over the Israelites. Jonah fled to the sea and Moses to the desert.

Right away, the problem with running away becomes apparent: there's nowhere to escape from God. But that hasn't kept me from trying.

All of us have different paths down which we scurry. We go as fast as we can, throwing up roadblocks to the love that seeks to enter our lives and transform them. My favorite form of running away from God was intellectualization.

Here's how it works. If I can understand something, I have control over it instead of it having control over me. So I spent much of my life trying to understand myself, my fellow humans, and God. I used to read books on psychology and religion by the truckload. I couldn't even fit them all on my shelves. I intellectualized what I feared. I became an expert on death and dying and even taught classes to help other people deal with it. That way I could avoid it. I could handle suffering as a concept, but not if it hurt me.

The beauty of this intellectual approach is that it kept me away from the sticky stuff of feeling. I don't mind feeling good, of course. I would be delighted to go around loving everyone all the time, dispensing benevolence and good works. Joy is fine too; I'm all for it. And I'm all for a God who deals out these warm fuzzies.

But I find myself instead often hating people, being jealous of those who have more than I do and guilty about those who have less. I get anxious, fearful, and angry, none of which I enjoy at all. I always avoided hospitals and felt suffocated visiting my parents in a nursing home. I didn't like to see the suffering and pain in others' lives and I slammed the door on my own. I couldn't trust a God who seemed to deal pain and pleasure in equal measure.

If I could just understand how God worked, then maybe God and I could get something going, I figured. I tried and tried. I read metaphysics; I pondered unanswerable questions, to my husband's amazement and frustration (he is a practical sort and would rather deal with motors that don't work or at least questions with answers). Like Saul when God wanted him to be king of Israel, I hid myself in the baggage. I thought my mental searching would bring me answers, but it only buried me deeper in questions. And it took me further from God.

One night in the bathtub I was thinking about a quotation from Gandhi, which a friend had sent me on a card. It said, "If you want something really important to be done, you must not merely satisfy the reason, you must move the heart. The appeal to reason is more to the head, but the penetration of the heart comes from suffering. It opens the inner understanding."[2]

This was not a new idea. In fact I had written a paper in college on the redemptive value of suffering. But it was just an idea. I had no intention of doing any opening or suffering if I could possibly avoid it. Suffering was one of my problems with Christianity. I had always hated the crucifixes in the Catholic hospital, with the red-painted drops of Jesus' blood dripping down his body. Any God who had planned such a thing made no sense to me.

While I sat there in my bathtub, a line popped into my head: "I don't mind suffering as long as it doesn't hurt." There I was—my inner defenses were just as bare as my body in the tub. I could embrace a concept while avoiding the experience. As though someone had shone a spotlight upon me, I saw myself clearly, all the running away over the years, all the evasions and shortcuts, the quick turns into the easy way out when things started getting uncomfortable.

And what I saw was that God in mercy had tracked me down to a place from which I could not run, at least not without a towel. God was saying to me that I can't be fully alive by experiencing only half of life, the easy and pleasant part. When I am willing to open my heart to it all, then my heart comes alive. When I run away it's my own life I leave behind. I can't study God to find him; I have to let God hold me in his embrace. And that scares me. And it often hurts. And it makes me alive.

God holds all the cards in this game, having made up the rules. If I choose to play with God, God automatically wins, having drawn me into his life and the fullness of my own. If I choose not to, playing my own game with my own rules, I lose, because God has the only game in town.

Poet Anne Sexton says this beautifully in *The Awful Rowing Toward God*. She imagines playing poker with God on the beach:

> He calls me.
> I win because I hold a royal straight flush.
> He wins because He holds five aces.
> A wild card had been announced
>   but I had not heard it
>   being in such a state of awe
>   when He took out the cards and dealt.
> As he plunks down His five aces
>   and I sit grinning at my royal flush,

He starts to laugh,
the laughter rolling like a hoop out of
     his mouth
     and into mine,
and such laughter that He doubles right over me
laughing a Rejoice-Chorus at our
     two triumphs.[3]

CHAPTER FOUR

The Obstacle Course in the World

As though our own resistance to God weren't enough, the world we live in throws up enough obstacles to daunt a corps of spiritual marines.

The world has a whole different set of rules and rewards from those of the spiritual life. We learn the world's games in school. We hear the world's judgments from our friends and our enemies. We see its rewards on television. We practice its standards at work. We can even learn them at church.

Since the everyday world is where we live, its noise and its motion fill our ears, our eyes, and our minds.

It's hard to stop and evaluate, to listen for the still, small voice of God. Often we don't bother; we really are too busy.

God knows this, doesn't he? God knows we face all this static and interference, so why doesn't God speak up in a voice of thunder, appear in our living rooms, write "I AM" in the heavens? Why does God put up with the gospel delivered according to Jimmy Swaggart, or Jim and Tammy Faye Bakker? Why does God plunk us into this worldly maze, knowing we will scurry like laboratory rats down every blind alley we find?

If God made me for eternity, why am I always scrambling to meet deadlines, gulping down the moments without tasting them? Deep down, what I'm really saying is, *"Why does God make finding him so hard?"*

I think the answer has to do with making choices and what happens to us in the process. God created me but gave me the freedom to shape my life according to the choices I make as I live through each moment. Nobody, not even God, can tell me that the alleys I scurry down are blind because I won't believe it until I get to the end of each one.

Like most parents, I've learned this from trying to raise my own children. I point out to them the mistakes I've made to prevent them from making the same ones. They don't listen, but that doesn't keep me from trying. Every day I spoon out a dose of Mama's Wisdom and they roll their eyes to the heavens.

God has more sense. And experience. I'd think that *anyone* would listen to a voice of thunder, a personal appearance from the clouds. God knows better! Look at the Israelites in the desert, whining that they wanted to go back to slavery in Egypt rather than to follow the pillar of fire and the cloud through the desert.

Look at Adam and Eve who lived in the Paradise we think we all long for, with all their needs supplied, completely loved and secure, in union with God. They found it to be nice and all that, but they just wanted this one more little thing: to be like God himself.

Look at what happened to Jesus when he said, "I am the Way, the Truth and the Life." God *did* made a personal appearance in Jesus, but like the people in Jesus' hometown, we can't see him in what is familiar. Jesus wasn't the Messiah they expected, and his message of self-giving love—obedience to God—wasn't what they wanted to hear. We in the modern world don't like it much either. We prefer getting to giving and control over surrender.

The folks in Galilee said more or less, "Hey, who does this guy think he's kidding when he says he's the son of God? We know his family, the parents, brothers, sisters. He's a carpenter, and a carpenter can't be the Messiah." Interestingly, Jesus could do no mighty works in that town, the Gospel tells us. God doesn't force himself on those who refuse. Not then; not now.

God enjoys irony, it seems. God has given us all the answers about how to find what we need for a full and joyful life, knowing full well we won't listen. What a crazy idea, creating the world and giving us the controls. Like ten-year-olds each offered a new red Ferrari, we take off for the horizon.

After years of weaving down the road at dizzying speed, crashing and breaking down, we find we don't drive quite as well as we thought. We pull over to take a look at the map of human experience, and we say with amazement, "Oh, the road markers were there all along!" But it's too late to start over. We have by then arrived *somewhere*, whether we like the place at which we have arrived or not. We have become what we are by the choices we have made, the turns we have taken. We whine that *someone* should have warned us. At least God doesn't sneer at us and say, " I told you so," though I often think I hear a celestial snicker as I reach another dead end.

We are easily distracted by the side roads along the way. William Wordsworth wasn't saying anything new when he wrote, "Getting and spending we lay waste our powers." [1]

Jesus wasn't the first one to point to the futility of striving after worldly goods when he told the parable about the man who spent all his time building bigger and bigger barns in which to store his increasing harvest, only to find that his life was required of him the next day.

We know this from the beginning, right? We come into this world with nothing and can take nothing with us when we leave. It's a given. We can't hold on; we're only passing through.

But what do we spend most of our time doing? Trying to prove this isn't true by getting all we can. In my case, each of us thinks, there must be an exception: *I* really *need* these things.

Like hamsters in their wheels, we run faster and faster to get more so we can spend more to get more. Turn on the television. People squeal and jump up and down when Vanna White spins the Wheel of Fortune and it showers them with goodies. Does anyone get excited about being showered with love and mercy?

It's easy to knock the more glaring examples: Rolexes, BMW's, Gucci loafers and penthouses. Ross Johnson, with his fleet of airplanes and celebrities. He may have been leading the barbarians at the gate, but the rest of us are behind only by degree. Donald Trump is too much with us, but we love to read about him because it makes our own greed pale by comparison.

When we acquire a lesser share of life's goodies, we can tell ourselves we're lesser chumps than Trump. I have a handle on this, after all. I work only for what I need, not to impress others, I tell myself. Simplifying my life, that's what I'm doing.

But I start looking around at all the things in my home, and my mouth falls open. We own four cars for four people (but we really *need* them so we can all do our own things). We have three television sets, two of which are rarely turned on. (But we inherited one and one was a present, so those two don't really count). There are three boats at our dock: small for short trips and shrimping; medium for days at the beach and choppy seas; large for weekends and longer trips. Getting all these things seemed so reasonable at the time. It's when I add them up that it gets scary.

Why all this getting and spending, all this energy devoted to having and holding? Well, it's kind of fun. It gives us something to do. It all seems like a good idea at the time. It gives us a way to keep score on how we're doing compared to others.

When a rich young man asked Jesus what it took to inherit eternal life, Jesus looked at him sorrowfully because he knew the man couldn't do it, and he told him, "Give all you have to the poor and follow me." It's all there in black and white.

The young man walked away. So do I, carrying my possessions with me. Why don't I give them up? I fully believe what Jesus told the young man was true. But I, like the young man, don't want to let go. I am wedded to these possessions. They may not give me eternal life, but I have a lot of fun with them. I would rather live with them now and think about eternal life later, when it feels closer to the end and my wants aren't so strong. It's all a matter of timing.

My attachment to possessions also has a lot to do with keeping score. If I have more than you do, says the message of the world, I am more successful and therefore more valuable than you are.

In America we profess to believe that everyone should begin with an equal opportunity, but once we cross the starting line together, I want to be driving the red Ferrari. As Vince Lombardi said, "Winning is everything."

So what am I to do with my life? The world's answer can be found on a bumper sticker I see all the time, "He who dies with the most toys wins."

God has a different answer.

Even before I reach the end of the race and check around to see whether I have won or not, I can feel like a success if I am running as fast and as well as I can. I may think it a bit gauche to be valued for what I *have*, but I have fully bought the idea of being valued for what I *do*.

When I meet someone I haven't seen for a long time, the person usually wants to know, "What are you doing now?" "Well, I'm . . . er . . . ." I respond and try to put good things in the blank. When I send in my news notes to the college alumnae magazine, I explain myself by what I am doing. My obituary will tell the story of what I have done in the years of my life.

Being known by what I did was never was a problem to me as long as I had a job. I knew my value to the system when I was a teacher or a journalist. It was right there on my paycheck. If I wrote a best seller, I would be of even more value because others bought what I did, proclaiming my worth.

Earning my keep: it's the American way, and it's ingrained in my thinking as deeply as my name is. I'm not alone in this. The world values us for what we do and we keep score in its currency. It's very hard for us to accept the idea that God sees us differently.

A friend told me about going to a seminar titled, "If You Are What You Do, Then When You Don't, You Aren't." That's what happened to me: I quit work and suddenly I wasn't. Or wasn't anybody I could explain. My identity crisis lasted ten years.

When I couldn't explain myself in terms of what I did, I began to question who I was. I could hardly explain myself as a trash can emptier, dish washer, carpool driver, clothes washer, or dog feeder. Too small.

Saying "I think, therefore I am" doesn't capture it for me either, though it seemed to work for Descartes. Too big, too vague.

Being a writer doesn't quite sound legitimate if I'm not being published. No byline plus nobody buys it equals I'm no good.

Unlike the baby bear in the fairy tale, I can't seem to find anything that's "*just right.*" So what's a mother to do?

God tells me that I'm loved just as I am, that all I have to do is to love God in return. Having bought the world's message that I am to be a human *doing* rather than a human *being*, I have a real problem with this. Like most things God has said, it's too wonderful for me to believe. I have to try hard to complicate it.

Those of us who live in the twentieth century have grown up with a particular obstacle to believing in God. We are heirs to the scientific revolution which began in the late Renaissance and really took off in the century before ours. People observed the natural world and made incredible discoveries about how it worked, and about how to control it, and then decided that they knew it all.

Biologist Charles Darwin fractured religious tradition by observing how species evolve through natural selection. Psychiatrist Sigmund Freud told us we act because of inner drives we don't even recognize. Philosopher Friedrich Nietzsche announced that God is dead. Sociologists say that our attitudes and behavior are determined by the groups to which we belong. Physicists now say that our old assumptions about the workings of the universe have to go.

Although I don't understand half of what these thinkers have said, I have learned about scientific method.

Its assumption is that what is measurable, repeatable, and verifiable is real. An experiment whose results no one else can duplicate is considered invalid.

What happens to belief in God when we adopt this view of reality? If I can't demonstrate God's existence to others, or even to myself, how can I believe in God? There have been many efforts throughout history to prove the existence of God, but never before has the assumption been universal that only what we can prove and measure is real. We have tossed out mystery on its ear.

Faith involves taking the data of inherited religious experience, one's own observation of the world, the witness of other people, and then—realizing I still can't prove anything—taking a giant leap into the unknown, making a personal decision whether to believe in God or not. Not so with the law of gravity. Both God and gravity operate just as well whether I believe in them or not. I'm the one who falls when I ignore them.

The scientific era challenges the ideas of God as handed down in the Bible. Many people feel they're faced with an either/or choice: either I believe the biblical cosmology which says that God and heaven are "up," or I believe the photographs from outer space. Either I believe the world was created in a week and that I am literally descended from Adam and Eve, or I embrace Darwin and revise my family tree. Every embrace of a scientific perspective seems to demand that we throw out God.

This either/or thinking has caused a gulf between Biblical fundamentalists and scientific-minded people. In the sixteenth century Copernicus was excommunicated by the Roman Catholic Church for his observation that the sun instead of the earth is the center of the solar system. Four hundred years later, the sun and not the earth is still the center of the solar system, and even the church admitted Copernicus was right.

Even in this century, a Tennessee schoolteacher, John T. Scopes, was brought to trial for presenting the theory of evolution to his students. Many people still insist he was wrong and that schools should teach that we are descended from Adam and Eve.

One group can't let go of traditional ideas of God because they fear this will mean abandoning God himself. Many others do abandon God because they think belief means abandoning their reason and power of observation.

I find I can't buy any of the pieces. Most truths about God are revealed in paradoxes. Paradoxes are hard. They don't fit into neat categories, either this or that. Take Jesus. He's fully God and fully man. How can this be if God is eternal, perfect, immeasurable, and mysterious, and if humans are temporal, limited, sinful, knowable? Over the centuries different factions in the church have argued in favor of either the transcendent or the human nature of Jesus because they could not hold two contradictory ideas in tension without being very unhappy. In today's world where we assume we can figure everything out, the tension between old ideas of God and new understandings of God's creation makes us so unhappy that we throw out the paradox and go on to something easier and more gratifying.

Although I am a Christian and believe that God has revealed himself most fully in the person of Jesus, I don't believe the Christian church has a lock on The Truth. Hindus, Moslems, Native Americans, Shintoists, Buddhists, New Agers, and people who stare at the sunset all have seen something of God, and I can learn from them. I don't have to insist that they subscribe to my beliefs; I don't have to give up mine, nor do I have to run away from beliefs that are different from mine. But I usually do.

The problem with the Christian-eclectic approach is that it leaves it up to me to decide what is valuable or not, and I am very prone to confusion and losing my way. My temptation is to reduce, to latch on to the provable, or to be rigidly orthodox for fear of getting lost. God is always bigger than my idea of him. This does not make me happy. I'd rather take a piece of him and run around shouting "Eureka!" than live with the mystery and tension of the reality of God.

Unfortunately, there's a lot of this shouting going on. Other people want to take their piece of God, run up to me, smiling from ear to ear, and shove it in my face. "Isn't it wonderful? Isn't it beautiful?" the Eurekans exclaim. "You've got to have one just like it."

I pull out my piece of God and take a look at it. It doesn't match theirs, although there are a couple of points of resemblance. "Well, mine looks more like this," I say, and hold it out tentatively.

They look at each other but they don't ever really look at my piece. They get out their books and show me how their piece goes by all the rules. Mine doesn't, they insist, though they still studiously avoid weighing it. They step back to see if I am convinced yet. I'm still holding mine, worn and a little dirty from being in my pocket so long. I've always wanted to find someone to share it with.

"But what about mine?" I ask them.

"No good, no good. Come on Wednesday night and we'll introduce you to lots of others who have pieces just like ours," they tell me. "We'll show you how to be happy. We'll make your piece look just like ours."

"But my piece is important to me," I object. "I've had it a long time. I got it from my grandmother when I was a little girl and I've kept it deep in my pocket all this time."

"You've got to get rid of it. It's all wrong," they tell me, standing close together, their backs straight. Their tone is more insistent. "Hand it over." They hold out their hands. Their Bibles are tucked under their arms.

I put my piece back into my pocket and turn around. "No thanks," I tell them. I start to walk away.

"You're making a mistake," they warn me, walking faster until they're in front of me again. They open their jackets and I see shiny badges on their shirts. "Army of God" the badges say. They are wearing sidearms, which they start to unholster.

I'm scared now. I start to run. They run after me, shooting bullets of righteousness. I have guilt burns around my ears. I dive into the bushes and they thunder on by. My heart is pounding. I rummage around in my pocket, terrified. My piece of God is gone! I feel around in the dirt. There it is, thank heavens. I put it back in my pocket and jam it to the bottom. I will never show it to anyone again.

The biggest obstacle the world presents to my relationship with God seems to be finding the time for it. It does take time and attention, like any relationship worth having.

"You always find time to do what you really want to do," the old adage says, and I'm sure that's true. But often I don't make the time because I don't know how much I need God. I don't know what a difference this relationship can mean in my life until I try it, but unless I try it I don't know I want it. Catch–22. Another paradox.

What it takes is setting aside time for reading the Bible, for prayer, for silence. Although this gives me great joy, I have a terrible struggle with it.

Everything gets in the way. The phone rings. The kids need me. My husband wants something. I think, "I'll just put this load in the washer and straighten up the kitchen and then I'll get to it." I have a meeting. I've got to do my exercises. The phone rings again. It's time to put the clothes in the dryer. "What's for lunch? There's nothing to eat in here."

Does this mean I have to get me to a nunnery to tune in to God? Sometimes.

I find that often it does take that. I go off to a convent for a silent retreat. When I can go into one small room and shut the door on the world, I regain a sense of who I am. I remember that I am created by God in the divine image, that I can find God's kingdom within.

I feel the pieces of myself come together in this awareness. I feel renewed and whole.

I go home, determined to maintain time and space for God. I do, for a while, and I am rewarded by an island of peace inside myself while the world whirls around me. Then the peace starts to erode again. Same old distractions: little things, nibbling away my God-centeredness like mice around a piece of cheese. It goes on until once again I feel fragmented and retreat to find wholeness.

I begin to get the idea. This is a pattern, and it's not just mine, because all the other people I meet at retreats are there for the same reason. Spiritual giants may manage to stay focused on God, but for the rest of us Lilliputians, it's a constant struggle, with two steps backwards for each one forward. Often we aren't even sure which is which.

I suspect that my rhythm of fragmentation/retreat/wholeness/fragmentation is part of a larger rhythm like the movement of the tides, the changes of the season. I want to be able to hold on, to scramble to the top of Mount Sinai where I will see God face to face and then stay there. But the glimpses I have are probably all I am ready for. Even Moses hid his face from the power of God. He too had to come back down into the chaos of the everyday. But even his brief encounter transformed him so that he had to veil his face. How would I deal with the IRS, I wonder, if I'd been talking to God all day?

Since the world is such an obstacle to a relationship with God, does this mean that I should renounce it and live in asceticism like the desert fathers, allowing myself no pleasures? Does loving God mean renouncing the world?

I think not. God, after all, created the world and loved it enough to join with it in the suffering and death of Jesus. If we renounced the world, where would we go? It may not be perfect, but it's all we've got.

Like all God's answers, this one is a paradox: We are to be in the world but not of the world. What this means, as I understand it, is that we love it as God loved it, in self-giving instead of self-gratifying. If we use the world and others only to satisfy our own needs, we destroy what we must have, as we are rapidly doing with the pollution of our planet. If we see others only in terms of what they can do for us, we cannot have any satisfying relationships. If we must have all the world's treasures, we condemn ourselves to permanent wanting. We must enjoy without needing to possess and control.

I don't mean that I can do this. I can't even love one other person unselfishly! If I could, I wouldn't need God. That's why, as Paul was told, God's power works through our weakness. Another damn paradox.

I would just throw up my hands on the whole business if I had not experienced for fleeting moments what it's like to be an opening for God's love in the world. In these moments, the veil falls away and I glimpse God behind the scenes, even behind such a prop as myself. It has happened when I held the hand of a friend whose husband was dying; when I told my daughter the truth as deeply as I knew it and she believed me—and so believed in me; when I've recognized what an ass I was for a thoughtless remark, said I was sorry, and have been forgiven. These moments give me joy, and it's a lot different from pleasure.

I think God wants us to have pleasure too. After all, he gave us sex. But he threw a monkey wrench into such pleasure. If I go after it as an end in itself, I may get some pleasure, but it's not so much fun as I'd hoped and I won't find true satisfaction. I'll always be incomplete, always want more.

If I give myself as fully as I can, I can know the ecstasy of total surrender—the joy of going beyond the confines of myself, of deeply sharing another's life.

Only with sex, I still want more anyway. It's one of those paradoxes.

CHAPTER FIVE

You Can't Get
There from Here

The spiritual journey is itself a paradox. It isn't a straight path from here to there, a march up the mountain where we find God at the top. It's more like being stuck, coming loose, then getting stuck again. As we move through time in the linear sense, the spiritual journey is happening on another plane; it involves finding God and being found by God where we are and then seeing in a new way.

Here I am, now past the middle of my life. I don't know half as much as I thought; the more I think, the more I realize how little I know. I haven't done what I imagined I'd do, and I have no idea what I may yet do. Some of the worst things that have happened to me have turned out to be the best, and the "good" ones the worst. The alchemy of living turns straw to gold and back to straw again. Much of the time, I can't even tell the difference.

I've wanted to be in charge, to set my life on a course and follow it. Now I struggle to surrender. I still fight the same battles with myself, and yet somehow I feel myself being led. I know I am growing. I am less rigid, more alive.

I stop and take stock. I've taken some wrong turns and made lots of mistakes, but I'm still OK. I'm not where I thought I'd be, but I'm learning to like where I am. It's not all up to me anyhow.

That's one of the two biggest things I've learned: I can't make it on my own. I need help. It's been very hard to admit that. I don't like to think I need a savior.

My other greatest discovery is that the help will be there when I need it. And that the saving has already been done. A story came to me the other night, just like a dream, which lit up this truth for me. I imagined I am in an elegant restaurant with sparkling crystal wine glasses and large brass chandeliers that throw a soft light. I am seated at a huge table with many other diners, most of whom are laughing, drinking the red wine with pleasure, sharing tastes of the smoked salmon, rare roast beef, tender asparagus with hollandaise sauce, hearts of palm salad, baked Alaska.

I can hardly choke down a bite of anything because I know that I have only a dollar in my pocket. When it comes time to pay the check, I will be shown up for the pauper I am. Everyone will laugh. The owner may even call the police. I can't imagine what I am doing here in the first place with all these people who are obviously not my kind.

I sit miserably through the meal, watching the others out of the corner of my eye, pushing the food around on my plate. Then chairs start to scrape, and everyone stands up and begins to walk toward the cash register near the door. I stare at the floor and drag my feet, bringing up the rear of the group.

A man next to me notices my distress and seems to guess the cause of it. "Don't worry," he says, patting me on the back. "It's on the house. The bill's been paid. All we have to do is enjoy it and be thankful."

The God I have searched for so hard is as close to me as my own breath. God speaks to me in the whisperings of my own heart and in the love of other people. I hear God when I can stop searching, worrying, and talking long enough to listen.

Trusting God's love for me is the hardest thing I have ever done, and I'm still not always able to. I have never had any doubts about the bigness of God. It is God's smallness, God's connectedness I struggle with. I have a hard time believing that God notices me, or cares that I exist among all the billions of life forms on this planet and in the infinity of space. Why should God pay for my dinner?

Trusting God feels to me like tumbling into an abyss. As I started my journey, I feared that at the end of the road the bridge would be out. Better to stay home where I knew my surroundings.

I could not change this outlook by myself. I did not learn it by myself. Had I felt totally loved and secure as a child, I suppose I would not have had it. But my childhood wasn't like that. Not many childhoods are.

My parents' problems affected me deeply. Not every child has epilepsy to contend with, but I'm not unique in my fears of abandonment. If most of us don't have childhoods filled with unconditional love and support, it could be that our parents had their own struggles and mistakes, their own wounded childhoods. Only in the Garden of Eden did mankind know untroubled existence, and we decided that wasn't much fun. Like Adam and Eve, we don't like dependence or obedience. We chose to make it on our own, but in the process we've been let down and double crossed, we've received some hard knocks. We have holes and bruises. We've learned to be careful. We've learned trusting can hurt. We hide our nakedness the best we can, not only from each other and, ironically, God, but even from ourselves.

Because of our wounded ability to love and trust, we rarely can turn to God without help. We puff ourselves up with pride about what we can do on our own, to show everyone how great we are, even though we don't believe it in our hearts. We can't get from here to there by ourselves. The journey to God includes helpers to heal our hurts, to point the way when we are lost, to pull us loose when we are stuck. We need mentors, friends, lovers on our journey. We do not travel alone. God never intended us to: "It's not good for [hu]man to be alone," the Creator says in Genesis. We travel the path of all those who have gone before and those who will come after.

Joseph Campbell, an expert on the myths of many civilizations, has described the journey of the archetypal hero, the one who is called out on a mission to face dangers, traps, and temptations in order to bring home a saving vision, a boon to his people.[1]

In differing cultures over the centuries these heroes—Odysseus, Aeneas, Buddha, Jason, Prometheus—have had many similar patterns in their adventures. They meet many of the same perils, monsters, helpers. They are transformed by the journey; their old beings are destroyed and replaced by a larger self and a vision that can save them and others.

Most of us don't think of ourselves as heroes, but if we are to become fully alive we must make that same journey, undergo the same transformation. We face many small deaths as we let go of the old, and we emerge with a larger vision again and again. We realize our connectedness to each other and to all those before and after us. To refuse the journey is to die, spiritually and psychologically. But sometimes we're too afraid to move and we'd rather stay in our holes.

Realizing that my journey is part of an ancient and universal pattern helps me connect my smallness to the bigness that surrounds me. My experience on the one hand is uniquely mine, yet the pattern of the journey is defined, like the steps of a dance. It gives me some sense of fitting in, of a meaning beyond what I can see. The archetypes of the hero stories are similar in different cultures because the journey is that of the human spirit, the psyche, the soul, my own included.

Campbell describes the journey as having three elements: a separation from the world, a penetration to some source of power, and a life-enhancing return. To find wholeness, each of us must undergo the same process. Many do not call the source of power "God" today, but whether it is called "love" or "creativity" or "beauty," it involves a transcendence of self. For most people the encounter is not a one-time event; our lives are a cycle of the death of the old and rebirth as something larger. To refuse to grow is to die, to shrink into a smaller and smaller existence, yet often we clutch to what seems like security and avoid the journey.

Dreams are often the bridge between our individual worlds and the larger human drama. They show us when we're stuck and they point the way out. Our dreams contain the same monsters the archetypal hero encounters, for our journey is his. Or hers. The female archetypes often follow quite a different path, but that topic would fill another whole book—perhaps my own next book. The hero myths will serve here for the universal human journey.

I do not remember all my dreams, but I have had some very powerful ones that pointed out to me as clearly as road signs a new direction for my life. I think of them as some sort of mile markers, signs of passage.

The first one helped me to quit smoking. I had tried to stop smoking many times over a twenty-year period, but I would always go back to it. One time I even smoked cigars. Then my dentist told me that an irritation in the roof of my mouth was actually a precancerous condition, and that if I continued to smoke, I had ten times the chance of an average person of developing cancer of the mouth.

I took that in, didn't say much, and went on home. That weekend my husband and I went to stay on our boat with another couple and do some fishing. It rained for three days straight, so we played cards, drank bloody marys, and smoked. By the time I got home, my mouth felt like the inside of a sewer, only hot.

I had a dream that night that my bottom jaw had been removed so that I could not talk. In my dream my thoughts were bottled up inside me, but I could not let them out because when I tried to move my mouth, half of it was gone. I woke up and told my husband that I had quit smoking. There was none of the old struggle; the desire to smoke was simply gone. I have never wanted another cigarette in sixteen years. The even greater miracle is that my husband hasn't either.

I had a dream when I began psychotherapy that I was in the middle of a house party, surrounded by my friends and having a fine time. I left the party and went off by myself. As I was walking along I came to a deep pool. I peered down into the dark water and saw white skulls far below, rolling around in the bottom of the pool, snapping and biting at one another. I was terrified and wanted to go back to the party, but a guide appeared and told me what I must do was to get in and swim with the skulls.

"No, no!" I screamed, but he insisted, and somehow I got into the water, sure I was going to die. After very tentative efforts I found I could swim there after all, and none of the snapping skulls actually came after me. Finally I could look down through the dark water and not be afraid. Then I got out, returned to the house where the party was still going on, and sat down at a table in a sort of breakfast nook. I looked out through the bay window beside me, and a flower bud just outside the window burst into a huge pink blossom.

The dream did point the way to what happened in therapy. I pulled away from my old attitudes and responses as I began to understand them. I left the party—my old ways of thinking and doing—and went off on my own. I met some painful experiences from my past which I had been afraid to look at because I'd felt they would eat me alive. I felt isolated, weird, crazy at times, convinced I would drown. But when I got through it, a new sense of who I am blossomed in me and I was free to experiment, risk, create in ways I had not dared before.

The blossoming itself was indicated and confirmed by another dream. I had been struggling with the manuscript of this book, tormented by doubts about my own abilities, whether it was all just a waste of time, whether I should quit trying to write and get a real job. I was out of town and sleeping poorly when I dreamed that my husband and I had been cleaning up a large room, stuffing huge wads of paper into a garbage can. Inside the can was nasty green slime, which covered the paper as soon as we put it in. Two cats sat on the wooden fence around the garbage can, looking intently down into the slime, only the tips of their tails moving.

I wondered what they were looking at and looked down into the slime myself. Something was stirring down there. I reached in and picked it up. As I held this lump in my hand, the slime began to slide away, and I discovered it was a canary, which immediately began to sing a high, thrilling song.

When I got home I was filled with energy to work on the book. I began to revise and rework, and within a week I had produced a draft that said exactly what was in my heart. I went in to talk to my therapist about the slime that was covering my creative spirit and found some more work I needed to do about thoughts of not measuring up, not being good enough, fear of failure.

Our generation needs therapists, Campbell says, because the myths that used to help people through these passages of life have lost their power in the modern world. We have rationalized them out of existence and must face the demons alone. Even the gospel can be powerless to move us. Even Christians find that their "inherited beliefs fail to represent the real problems of contemporary life." [2]

This failure of inherited beliefs of which Campbell speaks had happened to me. The Christian story as I had learned it had no power to help me when I faced the demons in myself because the story sat helplessly in my intellect. Jesus was no more real to me than Napoleon or any other historical figure. The gospel message was part of my life only because it was a part of my culture, not because it was a part of my experience. Jesus was not much different from Santa Claus!

What changed my belief was other people. Not evangelists, ministers, or those who were out to convert me, but those who loved me. And some who tempted me, who made me come alive, step across my boundaries. When I was most desperate, most defenseless, God could touch me, not when I was safe inside my own attempts at self-righteousness.

Campbell describes the hero's call to adventure as beginning often with a blunder, a seemingly chance event which begins the transformation. For me this was an involvement with another man, which happened when my daughter Florence was a baby. Feeling stuck at home with baby food and diapers, I was excited when I was called for service on the grand jury. I was glad to be out in the world where things were happening.

Jury service lasted three months, and during that time I was flattered by the obvious admiration of a very attractive fellow juror. I would watch him out of the corner of my eye and find him watching me and smiling.

One day near the end of the term we were paired up to inspect voting machines because it was election day. One of the polling places was at the beach, and we had lunch there in the process of doing our civic duty. That turned out to be fun, so we had lunch together again. And again. No problem, I told myself, just a little fun. But I didn't mention it to my husband.

Then the jury term ended, and I had to face the fact that this good girl was getting into something not so good because I continued to see him. As we were gazing into each other's eyes across the salad and he reached for my hand, my heart started beating so hard I was afraid he could see it through my shirt. I couldn't tell myself it was just good, clean fun any more, a harmless little flirtation. I panicked and swore to him and to myself that I'd never see him again.

I was disgusted with myself. I wouldn't have it. Nice girls don't do this, I said while dialing his phone number. I felt all the time that I was under a spell. I'd swear I wasn't going to meet him and then discover, as though it were happening to someone else, that I had. I was thinking about anything but archetypal journeys at the time, but I can see now that it was all part of the same process: my rigid ideas of right and wrong, my narrow self-righteousness, had to go for me to become a real human being.

Campbell says, "A blunder—apparently the merest chance—reveals an unsuspected world, and the individual is drawn into a relationship with forces that are not rightly understood." [3] I knew I had come in contact with some forces I hadn't reckoned on at all. Unexpected giants had appeared, and they somehow belonged to me.

I lost my sense of control, of who I was, what I could do. At times I had the sense that I was not in my body at all, but watching it do things of which I totally disapproved. I feared losing my husband, my family, my self-respect, all that I treasured. I had not the slightest idea what I might do next.

The hero is helped in his journey by guide figures in order to reach his ultimate goals. For a man there is the meeting with the temptress, the goddess who is both life and death, from whom he is rescued by a helper so that he can achieve ultimate atonement with the father (who also has both a threatening and beneficent character) and return to his everyday world with his life-transforming boon. For me the tempter was a man, who both awakened me to a larger sense of myself and threatened me with the death of all that I cared about, all I had been.

My husband was the helper who pulled me out of the morass. So was a close friend. I confessed my involvement with the other man to both of them, before it turned into a full-blown affair, not out of honesty, but because I was so sick with guilt I could not function. I couldn't sleep and ate almost nothing but Rolaids. I felt split in half, good girl and bad girl, with nothing to hold them together. When my husband got over his anger, he was able to help me see that what was really attracting me to the other man was a terrible need for admiration and excitement. Had I been realistic enough to understand that sexual attractions are inevitable and do not magically vanish when one is married, I could have accepted it and moved on. But for me, stuck in my "good girl" mode, sexuality was a monster I couldn't look at, and it overwhelmed me.

But it saved me too. Had I been able to maintain my good girl illusion, I might have become a self-righteous prig, passing judgment on others who weren't so strong and so "good" as I was. I no longer had that temptation.

My husband guided me through my self-deception, so I was able to end the other relationship, and ours was deepened. He has challenged me to move from other shallow places where I've been trying to hide into the current of life, and I have seen him at times as both lover and destroyer.

I am at times hostile to his guidance. When he points out to me that I am homing in on one idea so that I can't see other possibilities, I sometimes act as though he were the big bad parent trying to ruin my fun, not understanding me. I complain when he doesn't automatically know what I am thinking and then resent it when he gets too close and sees what I am doing better than I do.

When I was in high school, I knew he was the right person for me the way a lock responds to its own key, and I have loved him ever since. But I have spent a lot of energy since then trying at times to make him into someone else, some ideal I had imagined.

I have likewise had similar ambivalent feelings about my therapist, the guide to the unknown regions. During my four years in therapy, sitting on the sofa next to the clock and the Kleenex, I saw myself struggling up a mountain, falling, sliding back, getting bruised, while he sat in his armchair, serene at the top of the mountain, uninvolved with my pain. He knew all my misery, my weaknesses, but I knew none of his. It made me angry. At times I wanted to get to him, make him reveal his feelings, while knowing somehow that I needed his detachment. I wanted to quit, yet I kept coming back, knowing I had to.

As I look back through my own life, I see other helper figures, such as those who show up in myth.

Campbell mentions the wise old woman/man who gives a secret token. I have found this helper in several teachers who have believed in me. Their saying, "Yes, you can. You are all right," was the talisman that I carried with me. The close friend who talked me through my almost-affair until her ear nearly fell off helped me through other passages as well, and I have also been a helper and guide for her at times. People to whom I have been able to minister have given me a taste of what grace is in their acceptance of their own pain and helplessness.

With the help of guides, the hero finally escapes the perils and makes it to the top of the mountain. What is it that one discovers there? What does the hero find?

He finds atonement with the father, apotheosis, or he finds the god within himself, according to Campbell. This cannot happen to the uninitiated without disaster, he points out, citing the example of Phaethon, the son of Phoebus/Apollo, who talked his father into letting him drive the chariot of the sun. The boy could not control the horses' mighty power, and the chariot lurched through the universe until Zeus destroyed it with the thunderbolt to keep the boy from burning up the world.

The Gospel of Matthew tells of the king who has a great banquet but his friends are all too busy with their own affairs to come. He sends his servants out on the streets to invite everyone they find there to the feast, in place of the chosen ones. Once the new guests are assembled at the table, however, the king enters and finds one man without a wedding garment. He has him thrown into the outer darkness for not being properly prepared.

Atonement with the father has a terrifying aspect. God is not to be taken lightly. A meeting with God shatters all preconceptions, all categories of thinking and being. One can never be the same again.

Like Job when he faces God after demanding to know why his self-righteous life is filled with suffering, we, meeting God, can only respond, "I have uttered what I did not understand, things too wonderful for me, which I did not know. . . . Now my eye sees thee; therefore I despise myself, and repent in dust and ashes."

I can't help but wonder: If the encounter with God brings such humility for Job, why are so many religious people a pain in the ass? Why do so many want to beat the rest of us over the head with their mountaintop spiritual highs, their "oughts" and "shoulds"?

I think it's because they get a glimpse of God and run off with it. Like Phaethon they try to drive the chariot which is too powerful for them. The Eurekans want to corral God into their own preexisting categories rather than letting the narrowness of their conceptions be shattered by God himself. Then they want to squeeze the rest of us in, too.

When I have been in the presence of people whom I consider truly spiritual, I have felt more than anything their transparency. They have become channels for God's love to enter the world, and they are noticeably shorn of pride, defensiveness, the need to control and to be right. The smallness of their own egos has been transformed by the indwelling presence of God, though, being human, I am sure they have their moments of smallness, too.

I can think of three people in my experience who really struck me with this luminous quality, though I have seen moments of it in many others. One of them is dean of the Episcopal cathedral in San Francisco and an author whose books I have quoted frequently. He came to our parish church during a time of great crisis. He spoke the truth about what was going on and did it with such a tremendous love that we could feel the healing power of God in all the pain. People were able to admit their failures without being judged or condemned.

Another is an older friend whose energy and love make me feel revitalized just by having lunch with her. I go off like a bird fresh from a birdbath, clean and bright and shaking my feathers.

The third is a trainer in Sewanee's Education for Ministry program, who has caused me to confront myself in frightening ways, but done it with such love that I came away empowered.

I find myself experiencing a love I never had before and an intense desire to tell others, "Yes, it's all true. All the love you long for is there, poured out to you in ways more wonderful than you can imagine. God doesn't give you these deep longings only to leave you unsatisfied. Open your heart!"

Most of us are far back on the journey from self to God. We have our moments when the mists clear away and we see the mountain top of God, but we get very lost on the way there. Sometimes we prefer to stay at the bottom and melt our God-given riches into golden calves to worship. Idols, after all, are under our control and do not demand anything of us.

We can't be happy with our idols forever, though. We tire of them and want others. We are driven to seek something more. Nothing but God will satisfy us ultimately, for that's the way God designed us. We have the whole map of human history to show us the futility of getting and conquering. We have the myths of all cultures to point the way. But we must choose the journey for ourselves. We can make that choice after we have somehow been touched by God's grace.

For me the journey feels at times like it is happening to someone else. I am more and more aware of the presence of God in my life and in those around me, but what I see myself becoming is not something I consciously chose to be. It is more a matter of inwardly saying yes and letting go, then observing what happens. Paradoxically, the more I feel God working in me, the more I am aware of my incredible capacity for selfishness, arrogance, and cruelty, things I could not look at before. The more I surrender, the more power I find. The journey of the spirit is like walking into a huge, dark cave while holding a torch. I am aware at the same moment of incredible brilliance and the devouring darkness, together. The intensity of the vision calls me away from the grayness of the light outside the entrance of the cave, beckons me not to stay in the shallow places. But I go back to the everyday world to tell it somehow what I have found in the cave.

CHAPTER SIX

Known and
Named by God

Life is a journey from God to God, I once heard a
rabbi say. The journey is a linear one, one day after another, from the fusion of two cells at conception until the
breaking apart of our bodies in death. But the spiritual
journey also moves through time in the sense of piercing
it, knowing the presence of the eternal in the now.

This knowing for me has involved a new way of
seeing. It's as though for much of my life I had been
looking through a camera that was slightly out of
focus. I could never make sense of what I saw. I kept
thinking, "This can't really be the way the world is,
all this beauty, struggling, pain, love and loss for

nothing but death. This routine of day after day, getting and spending. There must be some meaning, some connection to something beyond it all." Then, through a heart-piercing experience of love, my focus was adjusted, and the outlines came clear for the first time, sharp and whole and breathtaking. I saw the energy and love of God filling the world like music fills a concert hall.

I had to know brokenness first. My shattering experience on the interstate and the disintegration that followed left me feeling exactly like a pupa ripped from its cocoon. My everyday self fell off suddenly, leaving me stripped of all my normal means of protection, writhing and wriggling and totally vulnerable.

But that vulnerability didn't just leave me open to harmful predators—it also left me open for God to reach me. I tried unsuccessfully for a couple of years to get back into my cocoon, and then I had such an overpowering experience of the presence of God that at last I began my journey out of the cave. This experience was so powerful that, in my thinking, it divides my life into "before" and "after," like B.C. and A.D.

I don't share the experience easily because I realize that it can't mean to others what it does to me. I am also somewhat afraid they'll think I'm psychotic. But I can't pretend this experience didn't happen either. It was more real than anything I've ever known.

It all began simply enough, with a visit from my husband's sixty-year-old aunt. Helen was a person I had always liked, someone who enjoyed just sitting around to talk, like people used to do before television.

She was short and chubby, with black-brown eyes wreathed in droopy lids. Her hair was a nondescript brown, turned mostly gray. The joints of her fingers were lumpy and twisted from arthritis; she'd had to give up her crocheting. Her smile was bright, impish.

Helen had grown up in north Georgia, in a family where talking had been honed to an art as the principal pastime. During her visit she told me stories of my husband and his baby blanket, of the farm dog that grabbed the pony by the tail until he got his brains kicked out, of her years moving from place to place with her husband, a career Army officer.

Sometimes the stories would go on so long I'd let my mind wander off. But there was a comfort in the telling. She wove a blanket of the past in which the present could snuggle, knowing it belonged somewhere.

I wanted to tell her my stories. About my anxieties. I wanted her blessing on them, her assurance that somehow my life would be all right. I needed to know that I could endure as she had through a husband's battle with cancer and death. That I could face getting old, being lonely. I envied her strength, her serenity. She'd been to the places I feared even to look at and was still whole.

She listened to me. The strength will be there when you need it, she assured me. You'll do OK. Listen to yourself in your deepest places, she said. Search inside yourself for what is most true. Pay attention to your dreams. The guidance and the help you will need are available to you. You are loved.

When it came time for her to leave, I was sad. Our time together had been peaceful, reassuring. There'd been no need to entertain her, no need to perform. She'd come just to be with us.

On a bright spring morning I drove her to the train station on the west side of town. My husband had gone to work, and I'd left my seven-year-old daughter asleep at home with a cold.

I moved more and more slowly as I got Helen's bag from the trunk and helped her out of the car. The train was waiting under the platform, long and silver and hissing clouds of steam. I thought of all the other times I'd had to say goodbye to those I loved. My chest tightened.

As I handed Helen up the steps of the train, I realized, "Oh, I think I'm going to cry." I blinked, gave her a quick kiss on the cheek and hurried off, embarrassed. As I looked back over my shoulder, I could barely see her behind the sun's reflection on the window of the train.

I hurried to my car and hardly got the door shut before tears came from some deep place inside me. They poured out like spring flood waters through a broken dam. Sadness and loss and longing swirled through me till all I could do was rest my head on the steering wheel and sob.

For the first time in my life, I knew my deep longing to be loved, completely and unconditionally, just as I am. Helen had loved me that way.

The sobs slowed after a while and I started back home, driving without fear down the interstate highway that bypasses the city on the west side. I felt as empty as a once-inflated balloon.

As I drove along I was filled by an overwhelming sensation of love and light and joy which entered me as quietly and naturally as my breath. The morning seemed to glow, not just from the sunlight, but from the inside of things, the very molecules vibrating with energy.

I pulled into my driveway, filled with love and alive as I had never been before. I wanted to run, to dance, to throw my hands in the air, my head back, laughing.

Florence, my daughter, was on a stool in the kitchen, wearing her foot-pajamas and bathrobe, buttering her toast. Her eyes were still crusty from sleep and her nose was running. I grabbed her in my arms and held her as tightly as I could, exploding with joy and gratitude for the miracle of her life and mine, for life itself. I thought my heart would burst open.

She was, of course, more interested in her breakfast and looked at me with her forehead furrowed, wondering what was going on. I fixed her eggs and bacon, reveling as I rarely did in the smell of it, the grease popping and spitting. I served it to her as though the act itself were the greatest privilege I'd ever had. Just to be alive was cause for a grand celebration. I felt like I'd been living inside a dark walnut shell all my life, and it had just cracked open.

Once my focus changed I saw this vision of God's love in the world everywhere I looked. How could I have missed it for so long? People became a great adventure to me. I saw them all, even the most irritating, as God's unique creations. I didn't need to seek out those who seemed like me for friends, but appreciated the difference, the quirkiness of others. I appreciated myself.

Literature, music, art all opened up as they never had before. As Elizabeth Barrett Browning put it:

"Earth's crammed with heaven,/ And every common bush afire with God; / But only he who sees takes off his shoes." [1]

Discovery of the world as God-filled made me feel I was exploding. I knew what Jesus meant about the very stones crying out if his followers were not allowed to praise God. I wanted to tell everyone.

I began to photograph life through my new filters as fast as I could, afraid I might not see with the same clarity again. I wanted to store the pictures of God up in a spiritual album where I could view them over and over again, show them to everybody. I wanted the world to see what I had seen.

I learned that approach doesn't work, any more than forcing your friends to watch your home videos. Other people want to look at their own pictures. They see through different filters. They don't really care what I see unless they see it for themselves.

I came to understand that it's the seeing itself that matters, not the records of what someone's seen before. While witnessing to one's faith is important, it has to be done with the utmost respect for where others are in their own journeys. I can tell you of the joy God has brought me, but I can't abuse you with it, or say that you must accept this wonderful gift, even if I have to beat you over the head with it.

A person's life is changed by seeing in a new way; each person sees through his own eyes. The vision itself transforms the visionary.

Seeing as God does is active; one can no longer remain a spectator. The new way of seeing involves loving what I see, knowing its brokenness, even its ugliness, knowing my own, and knowing that I am loved.

God's grace lets me see myself as God does, nothing hidden or tidied up. For most of my life I had tried to look at myself the same way I do when I stand in front of a mirror, stomach in, chest out, head turned at the best angle. God catches me at unexpected moments, and says, "Look!" There I am, my self-indulgent appetites and ways sticking out like my stomach. But God delights in me. I don't know whether to laugh or cry.

I cannot imagine why God wants to get involved with me. I am really not God's type. I had always preferred to read about God and let God stay in heaven, wherever that was. I had stayed in the self-constructed cocoon of my intellect, safe and secure and buffered, a bundle of the potential person I was created to be.

But a pupa can't stay in a cocoon unless it's dead, and neither could I. Grow or die seems to be one of the basic rules of nature. The life energy that draws us into wholeness, into relationship with God and with one another cannot be bottled up without disaster.

The intense feeling I had after putting Helen on the train didn't last at that level, of course. I do not still get up every morning thanking God for the chance to fry eggs. But things have never been quite the same either. I have met that deep joy at the heart of things. Even when I can't see it or feel it, I know it is there, there at the heart of me and all life. I am reminded of Samuel Taylor Coleridge's ancient mariner after all his trials, blessing the sea snakes. When he did that, recognizing a loving connectedness with the rest of creation, the albatross which had symbolized his curse fell from around his neck.

I have spent a lot of time looking back to that morning at the train station, trying to understand what it was all about. I wanted a rational explanation. I have found instead that I have been opened to mystery.

I became interested in accounts of mystical experiences described by other people. I found a particular correspondence to my own in the accounts of people who have been technically dead and have been brought back to life. I am struck by the descriptions of intense light, love, and a sense of returning to what is very familiar but never before recognized, like arriving at a strange place and knowing that it is really home.

I don't base my belief in God on just that one experience. It's gone on from there. What happened that morning was like a tear in a screen of everyday life that let me see beyond it into what my heart then recognized as most real. That glimpse brought forth from me a deep inner yes.

My way of seeing continues to change. I am still nervous about interstate highways, but I can drive on them. I'm still afraid of heights, but I no longer fear an abyss. But no longer do I feel utterly alone, an indifferent blip in an uncaring universe. I know as deeply as I can know anything that there is an ultimate reality beyond our daily existence and yet interpenetrated with it like the air we breathe.

I know as well that the greatest power in life is love, a love so powerful, like the sun, that we can only know a shadow of it as it breaks into our lives.

In his autobiography, *The Sacred Journey*, Frederick Buechner describes a similar life-changing experience of seeing. It happened to him in the Army. Buechner was sitting in a cold drizzle near Anniston, Alabama, eating supper out of a mess kit. Another soldier had left a turnip uneaten, and Buechner, still hungry, asked if he could have it. The soldier tossed it to him, but he missed the catch and it landed in the mud.

Buechner writes: " . . . I wanted it so badly that I picked it up and started eating it anyway, mud and all. And then, as I ate it, time deepened and slowed down again. With a lurch of the heart that is real to me still, I saw suddenly almost as if from beyond time altogether, that not only was the turnip good, but the mud was good too, even the drizzle and cold were good, even the Army that I had dreaded for months. Sitting there in the Alabama winter with my mouth full of cold turnip and mud, I could see at least for a moment how if you ever took truly to heart the ultimate goodness and joy of things, even at their bleakest, the need to praise someone or something for it would be so great that you might even have to go out and speak of it to the birds of the air." [2]

I recognized other reflections of my own experience in all kinds of places. I saw it in the paintings of Vincent Van Gogh. There it was, that convulsive, transforming energy I had seen, captured in the twisting, writhing power of his art. I had felt myself as he did—a little crazy; I was looking for soul mates. Van Gogh writes in one of his letters: "Oh, my dear comrades, let us crazy ones have delight in our eyesight in spite of everything, yes, let's!" [3] While I don't want to part with my ear (like Van Gogh), I never want to go back to being sane, reasonable, careful, half alive either.

Poems I had read years before started coming back into my mind, and I would dig through college textbooks until I could find them. I was looking for what matched what I had seen, and I found it again in the poetry of Gerard Manley Hopkins. Hopkins sees the world "charged with the grandeur of God." He writes:

> There lives the dearest freshness deep down things;
> And though the last lights off the black West went
> Oh, morning, at the brown brink eastward springs—
> Because the Holy Ghost over the bent
> World broods with warm breast and with ah! bright
> wings.[4]

That was it. I knew as Hopkins did that "dearest freshness deep down things." I had found it in myself, and now I saw it everywhere. Another poet, e.e. cummings, describes it as a feeling of deep and joyful gratitude:

> i thank You God for most this amazing
> day: for the leaping greenly spirits of trees
> and a blue true dream of sky; and for everything
> which is natural which is infinite which is yes
>
> (i who have died am alive again today,
> and this is the sun's birthday; this is the birth
> day of life and of love and wings: and of the gay
> great happening illimitably earth)
>
> how should tasting touching hearing seeing
> breathing any—lifted from the no

of all nothing—human merely being
doubt unimaginable You?

(now the ears of my ears awake and
now the eyes of my eyes are opened) [5]

I'm afraid I'm not like the people in *Guideposts* whose lives are instantly transformed by an overwhelming experience of God. Those stories often seem too instant, too simple. The frail young girl survives a terrible car crash and devotes her life to caring for the homeless. My faith has always been a struggle, even after that seminal experience of God. I am many times assailed by doubts and fears and thoughts that perhaps it was just some psychological aberration, a short in my cerebral cortex. Maybe just an infantile longing for an omnipotent parent.

These fears are put to rest when I can find resonance between my experiences and those of others. I need the vision of others to affirm the yes at the heart of creation, the community of believers to support my faith. My old habits of wanting to earn my way, wanting to justify my existence don't die easily. I can manage to twist anything.

I have found the support in many places, particularly through meeting with a ten-person seminar group in the Education for Ministry Program from the University of the South. I joined one of these groups ten years ago, with no particular reason other than someone asked me, and I had no reason to say no. I am now with my fourth group.

We meet weekly to worship, study scripture, share incidents from our lives, and reflect on how God works through these daily events. It is just what I need: a disciplined way to confirm what I had seen in that breathtaking moment after Helen's visit. God really is there even when I fight with my husband, my shopping bag breaks and the eggs hit the ground, or my best friend dies of cancer. Our group has come to see God in each other and in ourselves.

I need a community of faith, both the larger one of my parish church and the intimate sharing of the EFM seminar. God keeps putting me just where I need to be and I don't see it until I look back and say, "Yes, of course!"

Because of God's Holy Spirit I have begun to change. I have found myself drawn to people who are hurting, caring about them, and feeling a part of their suffering. I work with the dying. I feel drawn out of myself, pulled by an energy greater than mine. Before I wanted to chalk up good works so that God and others would approve of me. Now I want to touch others' lives in a way that really matters, to penetrate the superficiality of daily life, to reach for what is real.

As I come to know my own deep longing to be loved, I can feel that yearning in others. Alan Jones tells a story of Mozart as a young man, running up to people on the street and asking, "Do you love me?"

Jones says: "It is a question we silently ask all the time. I see it in the eyes of friends and strangers alike. Do you love me? It is a question about resurrection and new life. . . . Our daring to ask it springs from our longing. Our repressing the question wells up from our terror. The Resurrection becomes a matter of choosing each other, of choosing life over death. When the answer to the question, Do you love me? is No!—when we treat each other as merely givers or deniers of approval—we have sided with death. . . . Do you love me? is the unspoken question shining in everyone's eyes."[6]

As I come alive to the pain and longing in others, I cry a lot more than I used to. Sometimes my children laugh at me. Once I even cried seeing a United Way campaign film. I want to tell people, "Yes, you are loved. All your deepest longings, the ones you're afraid even to feel, will be met, unbelievably so, with love poured out beyond measure."

I get angry more easily too. Sometimes at God. Sometimes at others and myself for the mess we make of the world, the hurts we cause each other. I used to shut anger off, censoring the fierceness of it because I thought I was supposed to be nice. Now I believe that God does not want us to be *nice*. Being nice all the time is deadly, phony. What God wants us to be is real, to be who we are as honestly and faithfully as we can.

I didn't think this up myself; I just discovered it for myself. Ireneas, one of the church fathers, wrote, "The glory of God is a human being fully alive."[7] I am becoming more alive. I can feel within me a "leaping greenly spirit." I care more. I hurt more. I know deep joy and then terrible doubt.

Not long ago I was driving back from Atlanta, along a country road, straight and flat and bordered with spindly pines. I wanted to get home, as I was bored with the scenery and tired of being in the car. The only thing that kept me from speeding through the area at 70 mph was the fact that I had been pulled over by the Georgia State Patrol during the first half-hour of my journey.

As I crawled down the road, struggling to keep the speedometer needle on 55, I noticed an old man shuffling from his small frame house to a chair by the road under a huge oak tree. Watching the cars was his Saturday afternoon entertainment, I realized. He eased down into his chair as I approached, and when my car was next to him, he waved.

I raised my hand to wave back, and as I did I felt a love for him so intense it pierced my heart like a spear, taking my breath away and bringing tears to my eyes. "My God, what is happening to me?" I thought.

Grace catches me in these unguarded moments when I am going more slowly, when I'm not too busy, too defensive to be open. I watch this transformation in my life almost with the sense that it is happening to someone else, yet I am more truly myself than I have ever been. While my life opens to God, I am simultaneously aware that I still like to be noticed, approved of by others. Like the kid on the playground who says, *Look at me!* I discover incredible egotism in myself in a crazy combination of the old and the new.

The difference is that now that I believe God knows me I don't have to hide my faults. I am accepted, redeemed, loved. I can quit trying so hard to look good. I still have a lot of the same hang-ups, but now I can laugh at them, let go.

The need to let go was shown me dramatically in another one of these unguarded moments. I was standing in front of the mirror in my bathroom, drying my hair, giving myself the once-over and trying to look good. All of a sudden I was so sleepy I could hardly stand up. "I'd better lie down before I fall down," I thought and went into the bedroom.

I stretched out on the bed with a feeling of great weakness in my arms and legs. Almost as in a dream, I had a sense of total surrender which was intensely sexual, an utter letting go, giving myself up. As I lay there, I was engulfed by a feeling of love, this time with a sense of pleasure through my whole body. I felt totally "known" in the biblical sense, a generative, creative power coming over me. Surrender was deeply peaceful and all right, not fearful at all.

Just as mysteriously as it had come, the feeling ebbed and then disappeared. I had no idea what to make of it, then or now, and was somewhat afraid to tell anyone about it lest they think I am having delusions of the being the Virgin Mary.

There are other biblical precedents however. After a visit from God, Abraham knew his wife Sarah and she conceived, though she was an old woman and had been barren all her life. She had laughed at the idea that she could have a child. God's knowing is like that, calling forth life even when all we know of ourselves is our barrenness.

God's knowing is holy, creative, healing, making us whole. God's knowing is bigger than the categories by which I name myself, bad and good, acceptable and unacceptable. God knows me and calls me by the name which he gave me at my birth and which he knows all along but which I have forgotten.[8] When I hear it I remember who I am and come alive.

When I can accept God's knowing me, I am freed to let go of control. It's as though I had spent my life clenching my teeth and holding my breath, but I can now take a deep breath and say yes. It's another one of those paradoxes that lie at the heart of every spiritual search: surrender to God is perfect freedom.

Paul Tillich wrote in a sermon, "You Are Accepted": "[Grace] strikes us when, year after year, the longed-for perfection of life does not appear, when old compulsions reign within us as they have for decades, when despair destroys all joy and courage. Sometimes at that moment a wave of light breaks into our darkness and it is as though a voice were saying 'You are accepted, accepted by that which is greater than you, and the name of which you do not know. Do not ask for the name now; perhaps you will find it later. Do not try to do anything now; perhaps later you will do much. Do not seek for anything; do not perform anything; do not intend anything. Simply accept the fact that you are accepted.'"[9]

Accepting that I am known and loved by God has freed me. I no longer have to justify my own existence. If I am truly known—all the hidden parts of me—I can relax. I don't have to try so hard. I find I am able to say, like St. Julian of Norwich, "All shall be well, and all shall be well, and all manner of things shall be well."[10]

After all, it's not all up to me. Thank God!

The Heart of Things

Settled in my spot
on the sofa
I watch the mound of fireplace coals
glow
with a hot, red heart.

Ever since I can remember
I've wanted to touch
that hot, red heart of things
but I have held back.

Heroes don't fear the burning.
Prometheus stole
fire from the gods
and he was daily torn apart.

Icarus pushed his homemade wings
too close to the sun
and tumbled from the sky.

But Moses saw a burning bush
and took off his shoes,
aware he stood on holy ground.

Barefoot, I watch the fire
beneath the crust of everyday
and turn within myself
to find the word,
"Behold."

NOTES

Chapter Two

1. C. G. Jung, *Collected Works of C. G. Jung*, trans. R. F. C. Hull, vol II: *Psychology and Religion: West and East*, Bollingen Series, No. 20, 2d ed. (Princeton, N.J.: Princeton University Press, 1973), p. 75.

2. Alan Jones, *Soul Making* (San Francisco: Harper and Row, 1989), p. 73.

3. Earnie Larsen and Carol Larsen Hegarty, *Days of Healing, Days of Joy: Daily Meditations for Adult Children* (Minneapolis: Hazelden Foundation, 1987).

Chapter Three

1. The Rev. Robert C. Carter, sermon at St. Thomas' Episcopal Church, Savannah, Ga., 1990. This story is not original, but Father Carter cannot remember the source.

2. Gandhi, Mahatma. *Young India* (Navajivan Ahmedabad: The Navajivan Trust, 1931), p. 341. Quoted by Eknath Easwaran in *Gandhi the Man*, 2d ed. (Petaluma, Calif.: Nilgiri Press, 1978), p. 162.

3. Anne Sexton, "The Rowing Endeth," in *The Awful Rowing Towards God* (Boston: Houghton Mifflin Co., 1975), p. 85.

Chapter Four

1. William Wordsworth, "The World Is Too Much with Us," in *English Romantic Poetry and Prose*, ed. Russell Noyes (New York, Oxford Univ. Press, 1956), p 317.

Chapter Five

1. Joseph Campbell. *The Hero with a Thousand Faces* (Cleveland, Ohio: World Publishing Co., 1956), p. 35.

2. Ibid., p. 104.

3. Ibid., p. 51.

Chapter Six

1. Elizabeth Barrett Browning, "Aurora Leigh," Bk. vii., l. 820, in *The Complete Poetical Works of Mrs. Browning*, ed. Harriet Watus Preston (Boston: Houghton Mifflin Co., Cambridge Edition, 1900), p. 372.

2. Frederick Buechner, *The Sacred Journey* (New York: Harper & Row, 1982), p. 85.

3. Vincent Van Gogh, *The Complete Letters of Vincent Van Gogh* (Boston: New York Graphic Society Books/Little Brown & Co., 1978), Book 15, III, p. 511.

4. Gerard Manley Hopkins,"God's Grandeur," in *Poems of Gerard Manley Hopkins*, Fourth Edition, ed. W.H. Gardner and N.H. MacKenzie (New York: Oxford University Press, 1967).

5. e. e. cummings, "i thank You God for most this amazing," in *Complete Poems 1904-1962*, ed. George Fumage (New York: Liveright Publishing Co., 1991).

6. Alan Jones, *Passion for Pilgrimage* (San Francisco: Harper & Row, 1989), pp. 152–53.

7. St. Irenaeus. *Against Heresies IV*, 20:7.

8. Frederick Buechner, *Love Feast* (San Francisco: Harper & Row, 1984), p. 18.

9. Paul Tillich, "You Are Accepted" in *The Shaking of the Foundations* (New York: Charles Scribner's Sons, 1948), pp. 161–62.

10. Julian of Norwich, "All Shall Be Well," *The Revelation of Divine Love, Thirteenth Revelation*, in *Showings: Classics of Western Spirituality*, trans. Edmund Colledge and James Walsh (New York: Paulist Press, 1978), p. 149.